Masquerade Politics

Masquerade Politics

Explorations in the Structure
of Urban Cultural Movements

Abner Cohen

University of California Press
Berkeley / Los Angeles

University of California Press 1993
Berkeley and Los Angeles

Published in arrangement with Berg Publishers Limited, Oxford, England

Berg Publishers Limited
Editorial Offices:
165 Taber Avenue, Providence, RI 02906, USA
150 Cowley Road, Oxford, OX4 1JJ, UK

Library of Congress Cataloging-in-Publication Data
Cohen, Abner.
    Masquerade politics : explorations in the structure of urban cultural
movements / Abner Cohen.
        p.   cm.
    Includes bibliographical references and index.
    ISBN 0-520-07838-1 (alk. paper)
    1. Carnival—England—London—Political aspects. 2. West
Indians—England—London. 3. Notting Hill (London, England)
4. Festivals—Political aspects. I. Title.
GT4244.L66C64   1993
394.2'5—dc20

The paper used in this publication meets the minimum requirements
of ANSI/NISO Z39.48-1992 (R 1997) (*Permanence of Paper*). ∞

Printed in the United States by Edwards Brothers, Ann Arbor, Mich.

FOR SIMON
Artist & musician

Contents

Preface

By the term 'masquerade politics' I refer to politics articulated in terms of non-political cultural forms such as religion, kinship, the arts. In most preindustrial tribal societies the entire political system is embedded within such forms. But even in the advanced industrialised democratic societies the major part of the political system is similarly hidden. This is why the study of the relations between culture and politics has preoccupied the minds of so many intellectuals, both marxist and bourgeois.

This book explores the dynamic relations between cultural forms and political formations in some urban cultural movements. The analysis is based principally on the detailed study of the structure and development of the Notting Hill London Carnival, widely described as 'the biggest street festival in Europe'. This Carnival movement is later contrasted briefly with the development of the Renaissance Pleasure Faire, loosely labelled 'California's Mardi Gras' and with carnivals in other cities.

Analytically, the study is a follow-up to my earlier explorations in the drama and politics of some urban religious, elitist and ethnic movements in Africa and the Near East.

My concern with the London Carnival started in 1976, after I had watched television news scenes of violence attending the celebration that year. It soon became obvious that the trouble was not the result of an accident, but of deeper political factors; that politics was in fact built into the very structure of the celebration.

During the following years I watched the development of the Carnival, intermittently interviewing leaders, organisers, artists, musicians and the ordinary men and women who participated in it, attending pre-carnival parties, fetes, meetings, seminars, concerts, gala performances, launching parties and exhibitions. I studied a considerable number of documents, newspapers, books, periodicals, and surveys that covered the celebration from its start in 1966 until the time of writing.

My brief account of the Renaissance Pleasure Faire in California is based on data I collected during three whole-day visits, one in 1979 and two in 1981, on subsquent sporadic enquiries and, with some local help in view of the distance involved, on press coverage of the event.

I am grateful to the many people and institutions that helped: to the leaders and artists of the Notting Hill Carnival for giving me much of their time in discussion; to the School of Oriental and African Studies, University of London, for making it possible for me to pursue the study; to the Social Science Research Council (now ESRC) and to Nuffield Foundation for small grants to cover expenses; and to the Centre for Advanced Studies in the Behavioral Sciences, Stanford, California for giving me a year's Fellowship during which some of the early data was processed. I thank Hakim Adi, Helen Hornsey, and Jill Selbourne for their valuable assistance; the many students and colleagues in Britain and the USA for their comments on parts of the study; Margaret Clarke for introducing me to the delights of the Renaissance Pleasure Faire; Gaynor Cohen for unstinting support and encouragement; Sara Cohen for stimulating discussions on the anthropology of art and music; the editor of *Man* for permission to reproduce parts of my 1980 article 'Drama and politics in the development of a London carnival' and the editor of *Ethnic and Racial Studies* for permission to reproduce parts of my 1982 article 'A polyethnic London carnival as a contested cultural performance'.

ABNER COHEN
Oxford, September 1992

Introduction

This book explores the drama and politics of some urban cultural movements. It is based on the detailed study of the structure and development of London's Notting Hill Carnival.

Urban society is characterised by population density and the intense struggle for economic and political power between different interest groups. Often a group conducts that struggle in the form of a cultural movement, such as a religious cult or the development of an ethnic identity. In such movements culture and politics are dynamically interconnected and study of them would shed light on both the structure of the cultural form and the political processes involved.

Many studies of urban religious and ethnic movements have been published in recent years, including some of my own. But the structure and significance of seemingly frivolous, playful cultural movements like carnivals, fairs and festivals, have been relatively little explored.[1]

The London Carnival was first held in 1966 in the form of a revived traditional English fair. It was then local and polyethnic, attended by a few thousand men, women and children, about half whom were West Indians. After a few years it became exclusively West Indian in arts, music and leadership, and national in scale, attended by hundreds of thousands of people. In 1976 it made the headlines when it occasioned a bloody confrontation between West Indian youth of British birth and education and the police, with

1. For a partial survey of the relevant literature see Manning 1983. For a perceptive discussion of the politics of international fairs see, B. Benedict, *The Anthropology of World's Fairs: San Francisco's Panama Pacific International Exposition of 1915*, Berkeley and London, University of California Press, 1983 and B. Benedict, 'International Exhibitions and National Identity', in *Anthropology Today*, vol.7, no.3.

hundreds injured. Over the next few years the carnival became a major issue for political manipulation by internal West Indian factions and external interest groups. During most of the 1980s it became relatively more 'peaceful' and publicly institutionalised, with a police band sometimes participating and the Prime Minister sending her blessings and encouragement to everyone concerned on the eve of the celebration. The radical leadership of the late 1970s had been silently marginalised and phased out to be replaced by moderate men and women who emphasised professionalism in the organisation of the event. More white people participated, contributing to a total attendance that sometimes reached the two million mark, throughout the two days of carnival.

The tranquillity was largely only apparent, however, the result in no small measure of intensive policing, of subtle pressure by the authorities and of increasing financial inducements from a variety of public sources. As the 1980s drew to a close, the increasing appeal of the area to young, affluent professionals and semiprofessionals, intensified police campaigns against local drug traffickers and dwindling public financial support led to the containment of the celebration within a strictly defined framework. All the time the carnival itself remained tense and its outcome each year unpredictable.

The carnival site is in Notting Hill, in the heart of the metropolis. When the carnival started it was a slummy area, notorious for drug dealing and mugging, yet adjacent to the wealthy streets of Kensington with their palatial houses, hotels and expensive shops, within a short distance of the City of Westminster, which houses Buckingham Palace, 10 Downing Street and the Houses of Parliament. The local council of Kensington and Chelsea, as well as that of neighbouring Westminster, was dominated by the Conservative Party and so were the parliamentary constituencies overlapping with them. As the years went by the area became strategically even more sensitive as the battle against drug trafficking intensified nationally and internationally, and as developers moved in, buying old dilapidated houses and converting them into modern luxurious flats that were eventually sold to white 'yuppies' who soon joined disgruntled older residents in demanding that the carnival should be banned from the area. However, the police, the local council and the Home Office each in turn protested that they had no authority to introduce the ban, that it was one or the other of these institutions that had the power but not them. Several

2

times the authorities offered to remove the carnival to a stadium or a park but the carnival leadership vehemently rejected the suggestion. Notting Hill as a place held a special symbolic significance for the West Indians who regarded it as, in the words of one leader, the nearest thing they had to a liberated territory – implicit reference to battles they had fought there against white racists in 1958 and against the police in 1970 and 1976. The carnival continued to exist, its greatest political achievement being that it had survived at all, in the face of formidable opposition and pressures operating to subvert it all the time.

The volatile nature of this celebration is not peculiar to the London Carnival. Generally speaking, every major carnival is precariously poised between the affirmation of the established order and its rejection. It is, in the words of Miliband,[2] a contested event. This is borne out by the histories of carnivals in Europe, the West Indies and South America. It is a fact which is hidden by the formal conception of carnival and by popular ideas about it.

As a blueprint, carnival is a season of festive popular events that are characterised by revelry, playfulness and overindulgence in eating, drinking and sex, culminating in two or three days of massive street processions by masqued[3] individuals and groups, ecstatically playing loud and cheerful music or as ecstatically dancing to its accompaniment. More specifically, the term refers to the long-standing tradition in many Roman Catholic countries of pre-lenten festivities. People are attracted to it because it occasions release from the constraints and pressures of the social order, generates relationships of amity even among strangers and allows forbidden excesses. Through interaction in primary relationships and change of role in masquerading, individuals recreate their self-identity and so are enabled to resume their demanding social roles in ordinary daily life. Thus carnival connotes sensuousness, freedom, frivolity, expressivity, merrymaking and the development of the amity of what Turner calls 'communitas', as contrasted with 'structure'.

This, though, is only a formal, 'ideal type' of carnival. In concrete historical reality, carnival is always a much more complex

2. R. Miliband, *Marxism and Politics*, Oxford, Oxford University Press, 1977.
3. The term 'masque' refers to the representation of a theatrical theme by a group of people and is thus different from the term 'mask' which refers to the covering of the face and/or head. In Trinidad and Notting Hill both are 'mas', though are distinguished clearly in the minds of the carnival participants. See D.J. Crowley, 'The Traditional Masques of Carnival', *Carib. Q.* nos 3 and 4, 1956, pp.194–223.

phenomenon, characterised by contradictions between the serious and the frivolous, the expressive and the instrumental, the controlled and the uncontrolled, by themes of conflict as well as of consensus. Although it is essentially a cultural, artistic spectacle, saturated by music, dancing and drama, it is always political, intimately and dynamically related to the political order and to the struggle for power within it.

This is not to negate the validity of the traditional meaning of carnival; on the contrary, carnival generates such a powerful experience and passion for people that it is always and everywhere seized upon and manipulated by political interests. Its political significance changes with such variables as the proportion of the people who take part in it in relation to the total population, their class, ethnic, religious, age and sex composition. Over time, the form may remain the same, but the event may change hands as it is dominated by one or another class or ethnic group and its political significance then changes accordingly.

The dynamism of the event renders its study of heuristic significance in the analysis of politico-cultural dynamics. The sociological importance of analysing the drama of rituals and ceremonials has been stressed by a number of social anthropologists, among them Gluckman, Mitchell, Peters, Frankenberg, Peacock and Turner.[4] The work of the anthropologist in such analysis is similar to that of a dramatist in the Brechtian tradition, whose play would take a familiar everyday event out of its ordinary ideological sequence and 'throw it into crisis' by showing it in the context of power struggle in society.

The two-day street celebration of the Notting Hill Carnival is the culmination of a whole year of activities by various music and masquerading groups who, together with their supporters and followers, have, over the years, become permanent cliques of friends who interact in primary relationships that are not necessarily connected with the carnival. In time, these relationships have become

---

4. M. Gluckman, *Analysis of a Social Situation in Modern Zululand*, Manchester University Press, Manchester, 1942; C. Mitchell, *The Kaleda Dance* (Rhodes Livingst. Paper no.7), Manchester University Press, Manchester, 1956; E.L. Peters, 'Aspects of Rank and Status Among Muslims in a Lebanese Village', in J. Pitt-Rivers (ed.), *Mediterranean Countrymen*, Mouton, Paris, 1963; R. Frankenberg 1957, *Village on the Border*, Tavistock, London, 1957; J.L. Peacock, *Rites of Modernisation*, University of Chicago Press, Chicago, 1968; V.W. Turner, *Schism and Continuity in an African Society*, Manchester University Press, 1957 and *Drama, Fields and Metaphors*, Cornell University Press, Ithica and London, 1974.

associated with a body of moral and ritual norms, values, beliefs and practices. In most cases the grass roots of these groupings lay in close-knit communities in areas such as Brixton, Finsbury Park, Paddington and Brent. Their preparations for the carnival are punctuated by series of extensive gatherings in fêtes, launching balls, seminars, exhibitions, calypso tents, gala performances and educational sessions for the young in, as well as out of, school.

These cultural activities by local groups went hand in hand with political activities on a more general level. The wider West Indian public was kept conscious of developments in the struggle of the organisers to obtain funds from various institutions, to get permission from the police and the local authorities to hold the event, and to overcome the objections, complaints and occasional attempts by the local white residents to have a ban imposed on the carnival because of the noise and disorder attending it.

The particular activities associated with the carnival were conducted within the contexts of wider political issues concerning West Indians in the country. Although these West Indians had hailed from different islands of origin, many of which did not have a carnival tradition, they had embraced the Notting Hill Carnival as an all-West Indian institution. Carnival came to symbolise as well as to enhance and demonstrate their corporateness and cohesion. Indeed the celebration was, during the 1970s and 1980s, the only all-West Indian corporate politico-cultural mobilisation to cross the divisions between island of origin, age and neighbourhood. West Indians would explicitly say: 'Carnival is our culture, our identity here in Britain. . . It is our heritage. . . It teaches our children who we are. . . It demonstrates our existence as a force to contend with'. A mythology of its origin has developed, with many West Indians maintaining that it was essentially African in form and content, while others dated its beginning to 1834, the year of the emancipation of the slaves, whence, they held, it started as a celebration of liberation and freedom in the Caribbean. This was a theme much emphasised in the 1984 carnivals in both the West Indies and Britain, which marked the 150th anniversary of that episode. Even the genesis of the Notting Hill Carnival became mystified, despite the fact that that origin was still alive in the memories of older carnivalists. Until about the middle of the 1980s, a white former community worker had been acknowledged by all as the founder of the celebration and as its leader for the first five years; but some of the leaders then suddenly discovered that the event had been first started by a black woman two years earlier.

West Indians in London regard carnival as a significant part, as well as an expression, of their culture in Britain. Its forms of music, dance, song, calypso poetry, masquerading dramas, the food sold in it, the sound systems pervading it – all these are West Indian through and through. There was a conscious concern about and preoccupation with the development of an exclusively West Indian culture. One leader declared: 'Without our culture we are nothing'.

This emphasis on a distinct West Indian culture was in sharp contrast with the ideology and patterns of behaviour that first generation West Indian immigrants had demonstrated in the 1950s. They had then seen themselves as coming to the 'Mother Country', had spoken English as their mother tongue, were Christian, and had received British education and imbibed British cultural orientations. They had sought to be accepted as equals by the natives and to be helped to integrate fully within British society and culture. Since then, though, the situation had radically changed. Economic, political, demographic and other social developments drove them to seek to evolve a distinct, homogeneous West Indian culture.

According to the 1971 Population Census – which was the last to mention ethnic origin-there were about 543,000 West Indians in Britain.[5] They were mostly young, with 62 per cent aged 24 or under. About four-fifths of the men were manual workers: skilled, semi-skilled or unskilled. In contrast, two-thirds of the employed women were in non-manual personal service, in managerial and professional categories. West Indians in Britain have come from various Caribbean islands, particularly Jamaica. Most of those islands had ethnically heterogeneous populations, among which those of African origin formed the majority. In some islands, for example Trinidad, nearly half of the population are Asians, mainly from India. In this book the term 'West Indians' refers only to those of African origin. Under the influence of the Black Power movement in the United States, the preferred term of reference became 'black' while most of the native population in Britain were called 'white'. Those terms were essentially political and not biological and were extensively used in the literature by both West Indians and others.

It is methodologically difficult to study politico-cultural devel-

5. See Select Committee 1977. The 1991 census covered 'race' and 'ethnicity' but at the time of going to press its findings were not available yet.

opments among such a large group scattered over different areas of the metropolis and the provinces, and institutionally embedded within a dynamic, fast changing, complex post-industrial society. This difficulty can be partly overcome when these changes are considered in the course of a study of the history, structure and dynamics of such a major cultural performance as the Notting Hill Carnival, with which they have been so intimately involved. The history and sociology of the Notting Hill Carnival are in many respects the history and sociology of the West Indians in Britain. This carnival movement can be understood only if it is considered within the context of British society, not within that of Trinidad or the Caribbean generally. Sociologically, it is a British problematic.

In this monograph, carnival is discussed as a two-dimensional *movement*, involving a continual interplay between cultural forms and political relations. Cultural forms are evolved to express and consolidate the sentiments and identity of people who come together as a result of specific economic-political conditions and at the same time serve to mobilise yet more people who, in turn, develop more elaborate cultural forms, which mobilise still more people. The various cultural elements in carnival are shown to be linked together in political action; but the event itself is a cultural form *sui generis* and cannot be reduced or explained away in terms of politics alone. Once developed, it becomes an intervention, not just an expression.

Culture is rooted in the physical, biological and metaphysical needs of men and women that can be satisfied only through social relationships. Culture thus refers to the values, norms, beliefs and symbolic representations and practices governing social relationships generally. Music, literature, dance and other arts are autonomous aesthetic forms, but are simultaneously also techniques that develop and maintain the cultural forms of social relationships. As Marcuse puts it, this dual meaning of 'art', as both aesthetic form and as technique, resolves the tension between art and praxis.[6]

Social relationships are, however, also relationships of power when considered throughout the extent of the polity. Even if we consider such intimate relationships as those between husbands and wives, parents and children, we would find that they have components of power when they are considered structurally throughout the extent of society. Thus husbands and wives turn

6. H. Marcuse, *The Aesthetic Dimension*, London, Macmillan, 1979.

out to be two collectivities whose relations are defined by a contract which is upheld and bolstered by the political system and whose terms are therefore contested. The issue is domestic if considered in its manifestation in individual cases but is political when considered generally throughout the extent of the nation state. By politics, I thus refer to the distribution, maintenance, exercise of and struggle for economic-political power.

The cultural is continuously interpenetrated by the political and is thereby transformed into ideology, whether of the so-called 'dominant class' or of a collectivity opposing it. Meanwhile the political is constantly expressed, articulated and objectified in terms of cultural forms and performances. There is no pure culture. There is no pure politics. That is why the analysis of the relation between culture and politics is so fundamental – and so complex. The main difficulty is that the phenomena that we deal with are simultaneously both cultural and political.

What complicates the problematic further is that these two components of social reality differ fundamentally from each other. Political action is intended and rational. Cultural action is unintended and non-rational. In political action, men use other men as means to ends, and it is thus a non-moral situation, in the sense that the question of morality is not relevant to it. In cultural action, men treat other men as ends in themselves, and are thus impelled by moral constraints. Furthermore, politics is a dynamic process and its formations are continuously changing, while cultural forms are more stable and their repertoire is limited. It is because of these anomalies, inconsistencies and contradictions found in the same reality that the analysis of the relations between culture and politics continues to be the central theoretical concern of the intellectuals in Western societies.

The Notting Hill Carnival, like all other carnivals, has been changing throughout its history and will continue to do so as long as it lasts. It will therefore be discussed here as a continuing history and presented in the past tense. For the purpose of the analysis, its history will be divided into five periods of distinct character: *1966–70* polyethnic participation and heterogeneous cultural expression; *1971–5* the domination of the Trinidad tradition of steelband music, calypso and masquerading; *1976–9* the appearance of British-born West Indian youth and the introduction of reggae music, with its associated Rastafarian symbols and ideologies; *1980–6* the attempt by the state to co-opt and institutionalize the carnival; *1987–91* the subjection of the carnival to an over-whelming onslaught from different directions intended to force it out or confine it within a strait-jacket. Nearly every period tended to be marked by new political developments and new cultural forms.

The first five chapters of this book are arranged diachronically, but the periodisation and the unfolding narrative are informed by sociological analysis. Some topics are exhaustively discussed when they are first encountered in the narrative but major topics are only briefly introduced in the diachronic sequence and discussed in detail in a later chapter.

Chapter 6 discusses the attempts by the West Indians in Britain to develop a corporate political organisation to coordinate their struggle against discrimination and oppression and indicates the processes by which the carnival is made to articulate such an organisation. Chapter 7 highlights the social dimension of Art and Music and hence their role in mobilising the masses to the movement. Chapter 8 presents patterns of communal leadership as pervasive processes through which the collectivity consolidates its identity and injects rational strategies into non-rational cultural forms. Chapter 9 considers carnival as a joking relationship which camou-flages a contradiction between alliance and conflict and gives a cross- cultural survey of the political potentialities of the celebra-tion in both respects. Chapter 10 contrasts the Notting Hill Carnival, staged during the past two decades by one of the most deprived groups, with the Renaissance Pleasure Faire in California, staged by one of the most privileged groups in the world, to exam-ine the carnival formula in relation to power politics. The Conclusion picks up the central problematic, dealing with the question of politico-cultural dynamics and then delineates the heuristic importance of the urban environment for the comparative study of cultural movements.

1

A Resurrected London Fair

The first period of the London carnival saw a small-scale, local carnival, which was a working class polyethnic event with a variety of cultural themes derived from different traditions. It was a time of full employment resulting from a boom in the British economy, which generated a mood of public optimism aptly captured by Harold Macmillan's slogan: 'You've never had it so good'. Those were the years of 'swinging London', the Beatles, Mary Quant, Twiggy, the miniskirt and a variety of youth movements of the 'make love, not war' genre, represented in Notting Hill at the time by hundreds of university students, artists, writers, US draft dodgers and others, many of them of the 'New Left' persuasion.

Carnival was started by Rhaune Laslett, a local community leader and former social worker, with the active support of a few hundred young men and women. She had been born in London to an American Indian mother from North Carolina and a Russian father. When she grew up she decided to identify with her mother's culture. 'We are a spiritual people', she said.

She told me that the idea had come to her when, in May 1966, she had a vision that she ought to gather the culturally heterogeneous groups in Notting Hill in a series of cultural events and performances as well as in street processions. During the following four months she devoted all her time and energy to mobilising the local population for the event. Her conviction of the importance of the celebration was so strong that she felt that, as she put it, it would be the most important achievement of her life.[1]

In March 1966, only a few weeks before the carnival vision, she had helped to organise a neighbourhood community centre called the London Free School and was elected its president and secre-

1. *Kensington News* (*KN*), 8 July 1966.

tary. The aims of the school were: 'to promote cooperation and understanding between people of various races and creeds through education and through working together'.[2]

In a series of statements to newspaper correspondents,[3] as well as in a magazine of the London Free School called *The Grove*, Laslett outlined three major goals for the carnival: to familiarise the various culture groups with each other's customs, to bring some colour, warmth and happiness to a grim and depressed neighbourhood and to correct the image of the Notting Hill area, which had been unjustly castigated by the national media as a den of prostitution, drug addiction, crime and political extremism.

Laslett was essentially a reformer, not a revolutionary. She believed that the best prospect for the immigrant population, whether black or white, was to integrate within British society and culture. The general cultural form that the carnival was to take was essentially English, that is it used the symbols of the dominant culture and ideology. There was no suggestion that it would imitate a West Indian or any other foreign form of carnival. It was, she said, a revival of the Notting Hill Annual Fair that had been traditionally held in the area until it was stopped at the turn of the nineteenth and twentieth centuries. Carnival makers would be dressed in the costumes of the earlier period, the old musical hall would be revived; there would be mock boxing, the appearance of Good Queen Bess, dart competitions in the local pubs and so on. Some groups would masquerade as characters from Dickens' novels; others would reconstruct in a succession of costumes and floats the history of Kensington. A whole week of nightly events was planned, and eventually performed, including poetry reading, drama, film, folk singing and dancing.[4]

Relentlessly, Laslett and the members of the London Free School worked to gain the support and active participation of a large number of people and local institutions. They booked halls, engaged drama groups, singers, dancers and poets. They elicited help from the churches in the area, and obtained a licence from the police. They also collected money through jumble sales and in contributions from local traders, particularly the antique dealers of Portobello Road.

The borough council of Chelsea and Kensington gave the

2. *KN*, 23 July 1966.
3. Ibid.; see also the references in the next note.
4. *KN*, 3 June 1966, 8 July 1966, 16 September 1966; *Kensington Post* (*KP*), 10 June 1966, 16 June 1966.

enterprise their blessing and promised a grant of £100 as well as the use of council trucks to carry the groups taking part in the street procession. The mayor gave his patronage and planned to dignify the carnival by his personal attendance at its opening and at some of its functions.[5]

A variety of considerations lay behind the council's approval and enthusiasm. It was, and had always been, a Conservative-dominated council, substantially representing the wealthy rate payers of Kensington businesses and expensive residential properties. The 1958 race riots in Notting Hill, together with the growing notoriety of the area as a den of prostitution, gambling, drug trafficking, overcrowding and house racketeering, and the publicised activities of a number of neo-Nazi groups in it had all affected the value of the palatial houses and blocks of flats in the adjacent streets. An improvement in the image of the neighbourhood was thus beneficial to the privileged party and could only be a positive contribution. The development of racial harmony would be a step in that direction. The race riots and the incitements of Moseley's followers had shocked the British public generally and threatened security in the area. The black population was working productively in the local hospitals, railway stations, industrial yards and businesses. There was no problem of unemployment; indeed, the economists of the day called it a period of 'overemployment'.[6] The council had done a great deal to identify the causes of racial tension and to eradicate them. An interracial committee, on which leaders of both white and black communities sat, was formed for that purpose. A full-time West Indian social worker was appointed and entrusted with the task of investigating points of tension in the field. In a series of reports, she was emphatic that the only cause of tension was misunderstanding and ignorance of one another's culture and lifestyle, and she therefore suggested the development of what she called 'interracial education'.[7] The council duly encouraged the initiation and organisation of some interracial leisure and cultural activities. At one time or another, a mixed Christmas party was given in town hall, a goodwill week was organised, a mixed cricket match held, exhibitions and essay competitions arranged. It is thus

5. *KN*, 23 September 1966.
6. Some economists argued at the time that a degree of unemployment was essential for the functioning of a viable capitalist system, to make it possible to shift manpower between localities and industries.
7. *KN*, 23 September 1966, 13 January 1961, 17 January 1964, 4 August 1977, 22 October 1967.

understandable that the council should be enthusiastic about the impending carnival. At the same time as pursuing its interracial activities it was reviving an old local English tradition as a framework for the event.

As the weeks of preparation went by, excitement for the event built up, with the promise of a cheerful, colourful public festival. However, only a short time before carnival week a bombshell was dropped – the mayor cancelled his sponsorship and withdrew the promised grant. He made the announcement in a letter addressed to Mrs Laslett, stating in vague terms that his action was prompted by 'certain information' he had received. He refused to divulge the nature of that information to the London Free School or to journalists.[8]

Laslett was bitter and furious, and in a lengthy article published in *The Grove* she spelled out what she thought the reason had been. She wrote that the mayor had reversed his position because he had been told that the Free School was a subversive organisation associated with communists, fascists, black muslims and provos. She went on: 'The membership of the London Free School is very varied and free and possibly embraces 250 members and we do not keep dossiers or reports on the political or religious affiliations of our members'. She complained in passing that the council had apparently instructed local schools not to allow their children to participate in the carnival.[9]

She also published a letter sent to the mayor by the carnival committee in which they stated that 'In view of the fact that a fairly large number of people of the community – singers, dancers, drama groups, commercial firms, churches and other voluntary bodies – still wish to participate we are continuing to plan the Carnival under the auspices of the Free School'.[10]

The carnival was duly held and was described by the *Kensington News* and the *Kensington Post* as a great success.[11] In a leading article after the event, the *Kensington Post* ridiculed the mayor and the council for withdrawing their patronage.[12] The paper went on: 'For our part, all we saw was an innocent, unselfconscious mingling of white and black . . . all intent on enjoying themselves and

8. *KP*, 5 August 1966; *KN*, 23 September 1966.

9. *KP*, 5 August 1966; *KN*, 23 September 1966.

10. *KN*, 23 September 1966.

11. *KN*, 23 September 1966, 30 September 1966; *KP*, 23 September 1966. See also *West London Observer*, 22 September 1966.

12. *KP*, 30 September 1966.

in so doing bringing a welcome splash of colour and gaiety to their drab surroundings'.

At one level the withdrawal of the council's support for the carnival might initially have been the result of the discovery that one or two political activists were in some way involved. The real issue was something more fundamental though. The mingling of white and black in the event was not so innocent after all, and the London Free School did not confine itself to 'interracial education'. For, even during the period of preparation for the carnival, school members were, in effect, organising the local working-class population, both black and white, for a vigorous, sustained and relentless campaign against the worst housing situation the country had ever seen. Neither the carnival makers, the council nor the landlords consciously linked the two issues. Like all other symbolic performances, the carnival had many different significata. The major impact of the London Carnival during the 1966–70 period, though, was to develop and enhance that united stand of the local population to wage a struggle for housing. The same people who came together to plan, prepare and stage the carnival, joined forces on the housing front. The carnival and the housing issue became invisibly intertwined. The council and the landlords in their turn sporadically fought against the carnival, as much as against the militants on the housing front.

The struggle for housing space is perhaps the most crucial political issue in cities all over the world. It is directly related to the struggle for employment, and for a large proportion of the urban population the acquisition of housing space is the major form of saving for the family. The difficulties in getting a foothold in the city are particularly formidable for newcomers.

When the West Indian immigration to Britain started in the 1950s there was already a shortage of housing in London, and the competition for it had been intense. There was, at the time, open discrimination against renting accommodation to black immigrants.[13] Advertisements for lettings in local papers, as well as at accommodation doors, openly bore the sign 'No Coloured'. Moreover, because they had only recently arrived and were not yet in secure and steady employment, and also because they lacked capital, it was difficult for immigrants to obtain mortgages from

13. J. Wickenden, *Colour in Britain*, London, Oxford University Press, 1958, pp.36–44.

building societies for the purpose of buying somewhere to live. The result was that masses of black immigrants were forced to seek rented, often furnished, accommodation at inflated rents. The 1957 Rent Act had removed restrictions on landlords and rents were duly raised on existing properties while newly formed housing development companies, seizing a lucrative enterprise initiative, bought old houses and converted them to flats for letting.[14]

Such conditions were most dramatically present in the North Kensington area, where many of the first wave of West Indian immigrants found employment in railway establishments, hospitals, businesses and catering concerns such as restaurants and cafes. Between 40 and 70 housing companies developed in the area to cater specifically for West Indian accommodation seekers, exploiting racial discrimination and charging exorbitant rents. That led to overcrowding, as, to save money, many black immigrants shared the same house or even the same room, the high density of their numbers imposing a great deal of pressure on sanitary facilities and local public services. The West Indians generally loved loud pop music and were used to staying up until the early hours of the morning. That had at times caused a great deal of tension with their neighbours; in fact it was at the same time used by unscrupulous landlords as a means of pressure on old white tenants, who were paying lower, fixed rents, to move away. Thus a housing company would buy a large building to convert to small flats and in order to drive away the existing white tenants would let rooms to large black families whom they encouraged to stage noisy parties. Life in the area became a nightmarish jungle in which housing companies sometimes employed thugs to collect rent and to unlawfully evict undesired tenants. In many cases landlords did not even reveal their identity to tenants and relied on third parties to represent their interests.[15]

By 1966, about 68 per cent of the West Indians in Kensington and Chelsea lived in rented accommodation.[16] Among other disadvantages, this meant that they were not eligible for rehousing in council accommodation which became a particularly acute problem after 1965 when work began on building the Westway, a long, massive fly-over, linking Baker Street with the A40. The new road cut right through the Notting Hill area and resulted in the demoli-

14. See also *New Society*, 1 August 1963, pp.15–18; *The Times*, 2 May 1959; T.R. Lee, *Race and Residence*, Oxford, Clarendon Press, 1977.
15. *The Times*, 2 May 1959.
16. Lee, *Race*.

tion of vast housing concentrations necessitating the rehousing of their occupants.

Though the housing nightmare affected blacks badly it also affected whites. There had been a core of permanent English working class residents, as well as significant concentrations of Polish and Irish immigrants.[17] Calls for joint action therefore came from both black and white residents who sought to organise their campaign against the housing companies and also against the local authorities. Their concerns were not only over accommodation, but also over public services and amenities.[18]

Scores of joint white-black formal associations were initiated during those years, under essentially white leadership. Though their base was broad they had narrow aims and served the limited interests of small groups and quickly disintegrated.[19] The basic weakness in the more serious of those associations was black-white tendencies to separateness, exclusiveness, estrangement and mutual suspicions and prejudices which were due to the lack of proper internal communication and of unity, and hence they also lacked the ability to coordinate the activities of members in the struggle to achieve their aims. Many leaders thought at the time that the problem could be solved by public interracial education as was ostensibly the purpose behind the formation of the London Free School. Thus Mrs Laslett wrote: 'The aims of the London Free School are purely to promote cooperation and understanding between people of various races and creeds through education and through working together'.

It is in this light that the significance of the carnival which the School promoted should be assessed. Most of the forms of music, drama, poetry, dancing and masquerading employed in the carnival at that period were cultural forms shared between West Indians and Britons and were therefore effective means of developing primary relationships among them. Thus, jazz sessions frequently attracted mixed audiences. It should also be remembered that the West Indians had regarded themselves as British even before their immigration to the 'Mother Country'. They spoke English as their first language and were Christians. What proved to be particularly effective in bringing about communion across colour lines was the interaction and cooperation between the groups during the months of preparation for the carnival.

17. *The Times*, 2 May 1959.
18. *New Statesman*, 18 June 1960, 5 May 1960.
19. For a discussion of a successful association see *New Satesman*, 18 June 1960.

Simultaneously, the members of the School were working together on more down-to-earth, material issues. The first enterprise they undertook was to conduct a detailed household survey in the area to find out who lived where, who were the landlords, what tenancy agreements had been contracted, what was the amount paid, what were the conditions of the accommodation and so on. The political significance of that survey was immense, for until then the landlords and sometimes the council had only been confronted by individual tenants or by a handful of them at a time making it an unequal encounter in which the tenants were easily outmanoeuvred. The survey, by contrast, revealed an overall picture and by doing so collectivised the issue and raised it up to a higher political and public plane. Once this was done the issue infused peoples' consciousness as one of common corporate interests, and more people eventually joined the struggle.

The political activities continued during the following years. For a variety of reasons, and probably in an attempt to clarify its nature and precise aims, the collectivity changed its name in 1967 from the London Free School to The Notting Hill Neighbourhood Service, in which Mrs Laslett was again in a leading position. The *Kensington News* described it as 'an organisation run on entirely selfless and voluntary lines by dedicated men and women who have turned a part-time aid programme into a full time social mission. . . . It is performing an enormous amount of difficult and extensive social work'.[20] The Neighbourhood Service continued its activities, both cultural, in the form of months of preparations for the carnival week, and political, in the form of coordinating and intensifying the struggle on the housing front.

The 1967 carnival was described in a leading article in the *Kensington News* as a 'successful failure';[21] the failure being a deficit of £155 in the budget, the success being the variety of cultural activities that were organised and the number of people who took part, including about two thousand hippies. The article stated that:

The Notting Hill festival lost money but enriched the community. It brought a lot of gaiety to Notting Hill, the street Carnival and the

20. *KN*, 8 September 1967.
21. *KN*, 29 September 1967. For more information about the 1967 Carnival see also: *KN*, 8 September 1967, 15 May 1967, 22 September 1967; *West London Observer*, 21 September 1967; *KP*, 8 September 1967, 22 September 1967; 29 September 1967. For planning the same carnival see *KN*, 12 May 1967, 4 August 1967, 11 August 1967.

international song and dance festival being particularly successful. At
these events the various national groups got together and mingled
freely and happily. It was a far cry from the sullen atmosphere sometimes associated with the area. . . . It showed just what a voluntary
organisation can achieve but at the same time showed up the Council's
own failings.

On the housing front the struggle went on. An article published in June 1967 in the national Sunday paper, *The Observer*
stated: 'A former social worker, Mrs Rhaune Laslett, runs the
Voluntary Neighbourhood Service Unit from her home. She has
passed on hundreds of tenants' complaints to an advisory panel of
lawyers, fought cases before the Rent Tribunal and the Rent
Officer and has taken proposals for new action on housing and
Rent Act reforms to ministerial level'.[22]

In 1968, the festival was called by the Neighbourhood Service
the 'Carnival of the Poor', because the stores and shop owners in
North and South Kensington would not give financial support, as
they had done in the past two years, and there was also the deficit
from the previous year. To offset the financial difficulty, donations
were given by the poor inhabitants, and from a collection from
onlookers along the route in the street procession it was aimed to
raise about £100. The hope was dashed on the day by torrential
rain, described in the papers as a 'tropical downpour', and only
£14 was collected. However, the local papers were unanimous in
expressing admiration for the tenacity of the organisers and the
participants in mounting the series of cultural and artistic activities
in the face of such adversity. The papers published numerous pictures to show how the carnival makers ignored the elements in
their gaiety and dance. One West Indian, pointing to the rain, told
a correspondent with great excitement: 'Man, this is like home'.[23]

In 1969, the carnival proved to be 'the biggest and best', in the
words of a local paper,[24] even though the thousands of hippies
who had participated in the event in previous years, were attracted
that year by a pop festival held in the Isle of Wight. Said the
Kensington News: 'The thousands of inhabitants forgot their housing problems for five hours and danced and sang on a merry jaunt

22. *Observer*, 25 June 1967.
23. For information on the 1968 carnival see *KN*, 2 August 1968, 30 August
1968, 13 September 1968, 27 September 1968; *KP*, 16 August 1968, 30 August
1968, 20 September 1968.
24. For the 1969 carnival see *KN*, 5 September 1969; *KP*, 15 August 1969, 22
August 1969, 5 September 1969.

in the streets. . . . The procession certainly united people no matter what their race, colour or religion'.[25]

The symbolic structure of the carnival can be summed up as having been that of polyethnic diversity within the framework of an overall unity representing a dominant British culture. Thus the first few carnivals contained appearances and performances by an Afro-Cuban Band, The London Irish Girl Pipers, a three-man West Indian band led by Russ Henderson, the Asian Music Circle, the Gordan Bulgarians, a Turkish-Cypriot band, a band of the British Tzchekoslovak Friendship League, a New Orleans Marching Band, the Concord Multi-racial Group and the Trinidad Folk Singers. In 1967 the Carnival Queen was a Norwegian girl masquerading as Marie Antoinette, with men and women from the American Airforce Base in High Wycombe dressed as noblemen and ladies.[26]

Yet all those bands appeared within an unmistakenly British – if not English – cultural framework. The first street procession of the carnival in 1966 was led by an English homosexual masquerading as Queen Victoria. The reports in the local newspapers about the carnival during those years list numerous British artists and bands. There were masquerading themes from *The Lord of the Ring*, from Dickens' novels and from the ordinary social life of Victorian London. Even the small West Indian steel band at the time repeat-edly played the tune 'When the Saints Come Marching In'. A report on the carnival in the *Kensington Post* euphorically referred to 'the revival of this Ancient Event'.[27]

Although the underlying political issue of the carnival remained generally latent and was the intention of neither the crowds nor the actors, the housing problem occasionally surfaced as a motif in song, drama and masquerade. Thus in 1967 there was a perfor-mance entitled 'England This England', described by the *Kensington News* as 'a musical parody of the housing problem'.[28] A year later there was a similar performance entitled 'Eviction Blues', dramatising the continuing unlawful eviction of tenants in the area. In the programme distributed by the Carnival Committee in 1967, Laslett spelled out the political significance of the event: 'The peo-ple of North Kensington, regardless of race, colour and creed, have a common problem: bad housing conditions, extortionate rents

25. *KN*, 5 September 1969.
26. *KN*, 15 September 1967.
27. *KP*, 23 September 1966.
28. *KN*, 11 August 1967.

and overcrowding. Therefore, in this misery, people become one'.

In 1970, towards the end of this period, because of growing tension in the area, Laslett cancelled the event only two weeks before it was to take place. The movement had acquired a momentum of its own though; other local leaders took over and staged the procession on time. A local newspaper gave the following account:

> By 2.30 p.m. about 800 colourfully dressed families left Powis Square either on foot, in lorries, or in various prams and push chairs and marched for about 3 miles led by Ginger Johnston and his African Drummers and witchdoctor. For over two hours the Carnival weaved through the streets and finally arrived back at the square, by which time Sacatash, an American rock and roll band, had set up and started to play. Music continued non-stop until midnight with Mataya Stackhouse, James Metzner and various local musicians playing on the stage. By 11.15 Ginger Johnston who had held the whole event together returned to end the Carnival with a dance round the square until midnight.[29]

Thus the 1966–70 period was characterised by cooperation across ethnic lines, notably between West Indian immigrants and British working-class natives. Many of the men, and certainly a number of the carnival leaders, initially married or lived with native British women. In Notting Hill there was clear working-class solidarity between immigrants and natives, both struggling with the local authorities over housing, schools, and neighbourhood amenities. Carnival was an expression, as well as an instrument of that solidarity. In the next few years, however, the situation was drastically transformed.

29. *Friends*, 2 October 1970.

2

Corporate Organisation and the Trinidad Conventions

The 1971–75 period saw a dramatic change in the character of the London Carnival; within only two years it became national in scale and exclusively West Indian in its leadership, arts and most of the attendance. Of particular note in its evolution was the anomalous development of steel band music in the heart of inner London as the major musical basis for the carnival and as a powerful symbol of its movement. The conventions of the Trinidad Carnival were systematically studied by the leadership and accommodated within the British situation.

These developments were closely interconnected with the economic and political upheavals that enveloped the West Indians in Britain generally and those of them who lived in the Notting Hill area in particular. When the economic boom of the 1960s came to an end and unemployment became rife the West Indians were hit hard, partly because they were relative newcomers, partly because many of them were unskilled or semi-skilled workers and partly because they were the subject of racial discrimination. The relations of amity that had developed between the black and white working class now gave way to tension over employment, which was whipped up and heightened by the prophecies of racial violence and of imminent rivers of blood made by the member of parliament, Enoch Powell.[1] The National Front, an extreme right-wing movement, gained an increasing following among white slum dwellers,[2] immigration regulations were tightened drastically and an uneasy situation developed.

1. E. Powell, *Freedom and Reality*, Kingswood, Elliot Right Way Books, 1969, pp.281–314.
2. For the history, organisation, ideology and activities of the National Front, see M. Walker, *The National Front*, London, Fontana/Collins, 1977.

The impact of these developments on the Notting Hill area was severe. It was there that the early wave of West Indian immigrants, especially those from Trinidad, had first settled, and it was there that, in 1958, the worst racial violence in Britain had occurred when, in a series of incidents, scores of white youths had attacked black residents.[3] The government and the courts had taken severe measures and the trade unions and various church denominations had strongly condemned the attacks. Their determined reaction, together with the economic prosperity and full employment during the 1960s, had inhibited the development of a negative reaction among the West Indians, but in the 1970s all the fears and bitterness among the black residents were revived.

A dramatic turning point, with significant consequences for the carnival, occurred on 9 August 1970 when a violent confrontation between the police and black demonstrators took place in the area. The demonstrators had been protesting against continual police raids on a West Indian restaurant called the Mangrove and their harassment of its owner, Frank Crichlow, originally from Trinidad. The Mangrove had been opened in 1969 to serve Caribbean food for both white and black families and it soon became a meeting place for West Indians from all the islands including among their numbers musicians, political activists and journalists. Situated in All Saints Road, the restaurant stood in the middle of what was to become the centre for drug trafficking for the whole of Greater London. During the two decades following its opening there were scores of raids on it, in which the police sometimes wrecked the place, allegedly assaulted clients and shouted abuse at them, arresting certain of them and detaining the proprietor.

The 1970 demonstration, organised by 'The Action Committee for the Defence of the Mangrove' in collaboration with the Brixton-based Black Panther Movement, ended up in Portnall Road in front of a police station where, without warning, it developed into a clash with the police. Nineteen people were arrested and tried shortly afterwards. A few weeks later the police and the Public Prosecutor thought they had amassed enough evidence to convict the seven men and two women. . . who came to be known as the Mangrove Nine. . . for allegedly organising the demonstration and orchestrating the violence which erupted at its end. The Nine were duly arrested and charged. Their trial, which lasted for

3. For details about the 1958 riots, see E. Pilkington, *Beyond the Mother Country*, London, I.B. Tauris, 1988.

eleven weeks, was one of the longest and most expensive ever to be held at the Old Bailey. The defendants and their supporters succeeded in turning it into an effective political demonstration, and in so doing elevated an apparently local affray involving a small number of people into a national issue concerning the oppression of Afro-Caribbeans generally.

Throughout the trial, a local organisation called the Black People Information Centre published a weekly newsletter giving details of the trial that it distributed widely in Britain, the Caribbean and North America. The whole Afro-Caribbean local community were behind the defendants and collected money with which to hire defence lawyers.

The trial ended with the acquittal of seven of the accused and short suspended sentences being passed on the remaining two. There was jubilation among the West Indians and a party was given at the Mangrove for the jurors, who were, on the whole, sympathetic to the defendants.

That episode was not an isolated incident but the product of ongoing political developments. In its turn it became a landmark, a symbolic drama in its own right, which precipitated further developments. The Mangrove was transformed from a local restaurant to an institution for community organisation, resistance and struggle. Ideologically it became a dominant political symbol. Its role in the organisation and development of the Notting Hill Carnival over the following two decades was crucial. It served as a centre where carnival organisers, musicians and artists met. Its owner, Frank Crichlow, who was one of the Nine', became a staunch supporter of the event. He donated generous sums of money to be distributed as prizes among carnival makers. His restaurant served as a base for teams of judges who assessed the mobile bands and chose the winners, and sometimes, as the bands passed by, Crichlow gave them whole cases of beer. The restaurant in effect became the heart and the nerve centre of 'Carnival Country'. During carnival time the Mangrove arranged festive colourful bunting for the All Saints Road and on the eve of the event was the venue for a children's party. Crichlow, who was regularly interviewed by the media at carnival time, shrewdly steered clear of identifying himself with either of the contending organising committees during the second half of the 1970s, though he remained deeply involved in carnival affairs. Meanwhile, his brother, Victor Crichlow, faithfully supported the carnival through the years, acting for a long time as treasurer for the Carnival and Arts Committee and later as director of the Carnival Industries Project also.[4]

Darcus Howe, who received national attention as another of the Nine, played an equally crucial role in the development of the Notting Hill Carnival. He had been known as 'the Hero' during the court proceedings in which he refused the help of lawyers and insisted on conducting his own defence. He impressed jurors and journalists by his conduct and cross-examination of prosecution witnesses.

He was committed to the carnival. In 1974 he became editor of the journal *Race Today*, and under his editorship it continuously supported the carnival, providing news and relevant feature articles about it. In 1976 he was elected chairman of the Carnival Development Committee. At times he played 'the iron' in a steel band and from 1977 headed a large *mas* band from Brixton with a very large following. In 1978 he led the *mas* band in a theme he called 'Forces of Victory' and a year later headed the same band as it enacted the theme 'Viva Zapata', in which he appeared in the eponymous role of the popular Mexican hero. He was a dominant figure in the carnival movement, which he, more than any other leader, helped to shape and radicalise. In the course of his activities he was at times arrested and brought to court.[5]

The Mangrove 1970 event was also a dramatic symbol of the shattering of the white-black community that had been brought together during the 1960s on the bases of neighbourliness and of joint struggle for improved housing conditions and public amenities. On a physical level the enormous A40 fly-over (the Westway) that had been built across the area caused massive dislocation and dispersal in the concomitant rehousing. At the same time a friendly white policeman who had been privately frequenting the Mangrove to eat and drink was later suspected of having informed about goings and comings at the establishment. Other white customers who had been welcome in the restaurant before were subsequently no longer admitted and the establishment became exclusively black in its clientele. During the two decades following the trial the Mangrove itself underwent several metamorphoses. At times it became 'the Mangrove Community Centre','the Mangrove Take-

4. See Chapter 8 for more details. See also T. Gould, 'The Mangrove Seven', *New Society*, 1979, pp.382–84.

5. See Chapter 8 for more details. See also C. Macinnes, 'The Mangrove Trial', *New Society*, 1971, p.1261.

away','the Mangrove Club', 'the Mangrove Casino' and 'the Mangrove Wine Bar' – but it always remained under the same management, who relentlessly manoeuvred against the odds, fully supported by the West Indian community.

For the police the Mangrove had always been a centre of crime, drugs and resistance – a continuous challenge to their authority. That was why they subjected it to perpetual harassment.

The West Indian reaction to those events took different forms. Their trust in joint white-black organisations, such as trade unions and political parties, was shaken. Leaders began to advocate the development of exclusively West Indian formal organisations and many such were formed. The ideologies, methods and policies of Black Power groupings in the United States were studied and, when possible, applied. On the whole, however, the development of an all-West Indian formal organisation was thwarted by a variety of factors and the various associations remained fragmentary and largely ephemeral.[6]

The circumstances gave rise to a strong movement for the development of an (increasingly) homogenised cultural identity to infuse West Indian consciousness, serve as a medium of communication between various sections, and evolve viable leadership in a variety of fields. Where formal, associative organisation proved difficult or inadequate, communal mechanisms began to serve as substitutes. A widespread and active search for an homogenous West Indian culture began in art, literature, drama, music, dancing and religion. A great deal was achieved, but apart from pop music, those cultural forms had so far affected relatively small audiences. Carnival, on the other hand proved over the years to have immense possibilities for cultural expression, and hence indirectly for political mobilisation on a massive scale. It could absorb and integrate a variety of artistic traditions and other cultural forms, and could involve different types of groupings in sustained activities within a symbolic unity that lasted almost throughout the year.

The 1971 and 1972 carnivals were rather poor. Communal tension had dampened the enthusiasm of the neighbourhood for the event. With the withdrawal of Mrs Laslett as organiser, the rehousing of many residents away from the area and the waning of hippy

6. For a brief discussion of this problem see D.G. Pearson, West Indian Communal Associations in Britain', *New Community*, vol.5, 1977. See also Chapter 6.

and other *avant garde* movements in Notting Hill, white participation and interest in the carnival diminished. Those whites who continued to participate had no clear concept of the event or grasp of its arts. The West Indians, on the other hand, had, initially under predominantly Trinidadian leadership, known what Carnival was, had the tradition, the experience, the arts and, increasingly, the motivation to seize on the event, revitalise it and make it exclusively their own. They did not long lack the organisation and leadership. A gifted young teacher and musician from Trinidad, Lesley Palmer, took over as organiser, and within four years he completely revolutionised the event and transformed its structure and content almost beyond recognition. As he was too young to have mastered the carnival tradition before emigrating and yet was dissatisfied with the current shape of the event, he went to Trinidad to learn and to seek help and advice. He looked closely at the organisation and artistic forms of the celebration, then returned to London to work on the 1973 carnival. In particular, he concentrated on the mobilisation of steel and mas bands.

The tradition of Carnival was itself, quite apart from its content, of great symbolic significance for the Trinidadians. It was originally celebrated by white master settlers in the island, but, after emancipation in the 1830s, the former slaves participated in it on a large scale and within a short time dominated it and drove their former masters away. Over the many following years the Trinidadians revolutionised Carnival by the introduction of new musical forms, new dances and new forms of masquing, that infused it with some powerful African artistic patterns. They persistently used it to criticise and ridicule the people and culture of the ruling classes, who, in turn, became alarmed and attempted, without much success, to ban it. They passed legislation prohibiting the beating of drums, on the ground that they were disturbingly noisy and incited rowdiness and banned the wearing of masks, saying that some men hid their identity behind them to commit crimes. However, the black population managed to circumvent these prohibitions by inventing ingenious replacements for the drum and the masks and over the years Carnival became an organising mechanism for protest and opposition. After the Independence of Trinidad, this political potential gave way and the celebration today is a national, government-coordinated, middle-class dominated, tourist-oriented affair in which men and women from different ethnic and social groups participate. To Trinidadians in Britain, however, Carnival remained the symbol of emancipation, resistance, protest and triumph.[7]

The steel band, which forms the backbone of Carnival, was a Trinidad invention. When the colonial establishment banned the beating of drums, the black masses began to experiment with various other means of producing rhythm for dancing. They tried the African shack-shack, bamboo sticks, spoons in bottles, biscuit tins and dustbins. They eventually discovered the musical possibilities of the 44 and 55 litre oil drums, initially made available by the United States army during the Second World War. They found that by heating the base of the drum, carefully beating and sinking it by about seven inches, then raising sections of it, the frequency of its vibrations could be altered and that by doing this and cutting the drum into varying lengths, a full range of notes and tones could be achieved. A steel band thus has a basic set of low tenor pans, high tenor pans, guitar pans, tenor bass pans and bass pans. In addition, a band also had an instrument called 'the iron', which was simply a piece of metal from a car engine held by a string from one hand while with the other hand the player used a metal rod to strike the iron and produce a special beat.

A band had a basic set of eleven pans, but this was often augmented by additional sets as the occasion required. In Trinidad some of the bands had over a hundred pans, but in London they had a smaller number, no more than fifty. The pans were hung up by wire from scaffolding and when the band played in a street procession the scaffoldings were either mounted on a large open truck or fitted with castors and pushed, row by row, by the players and their assistants.

Like Carnival, the steel band acquired in Britain a powerful symbolic significance. It represented something well beyond the making of loud rhythms; and like dominant symbols generally, it developed different, sometimes contradictory meanings. In the first place, there was a feeling of pride and elation at its invention and many of the leaders emphasised that the pan was the only new musical instrument to have been invented during the twentieth

---

7. This is a brief account based on historical literature. See in particular A. Pearse, 'Carnival in nineteenth century Trinidad', *Carib. Q.* 3 and 4, 1956, pp.175–93; D. Wood, *Trinidad in Transition*, London, Oxford University Press, 1968, pp.8–9, 242–7; E. Hill, *The Trinidad Carnival: Mandate for a National Theatre*, Austin and London, University of Texas Press, 1972. Further details are given in D.J. Crowley, 'Traditional Masques'; B.E. Powrie, 'The Changing Attitude of Coloured Middle Class Towards Carnival', *Carib. Q.*, 3 and 4, 1956, pp.224–32.

century,[8] and there were attempts in both Trinidad and in Britain to play classical music on it. At the same time, the pan, with its rust, rough edges and clumsy appearance was a symbol of poverty, a protest that in the land of plenty, where so many sophisticated musical instruments were available, a people should be forced to pick up abandoned shells to express their artistic feelings. The symbolic nature of the pan in that respect can be appreciated even more in light of the fact that the 'simple' pan was, ironically, more expensive than some of the major musical instruments. The oil drum itself cost little, but heating, beating, grooving, cutting and tuning it, had become a very specialised, labour-intensive, profession practised by only a few West Indian families in London. The final product cost about £85 each (at 1980 prices). As an average band in Britain consisted of twenty pans, the cost in the impoverished period of supplying a band with pans alone was substantial.

Of more direct symbolic significance was the transformation the steel band brought about in the people who played in it and danced to it, and the links that evolved between them. One of the leading figures in the steel band movement in Britain told me that 'the steel band was born in violence, it expresses violence and it inspires violence'. In Trinidad it was evolved by gangs of unemployed neighbourhood youths who staged night raids on industrial premises to steal the oil drums. When no empty drums could be found they simply emptied full ones, moved them to a hiding place, and immediately painted them to hide their identity.[9] The pans played the role of military drums in staging attacks against rival gangs from different neighbourhoods. For that reason parents, church and police had always been against steel bands.

The pan men hammered furiously over the steel to express their built-in outrage against past and present oppression, discrimination and injustice. Darcus Howe wrote that, after being outraged by a police raid on the Mangrove restaurant during the 1976 carnival, he joined one of the bands and spent two or three hours 'knocking hell out of steel' in order to restore his composure.[10] In a different context he spoke of 'the aggressive sweetness of the steel band music'. Thus, for the players the music was very much the sound of protest, a loud and noisy sound of scores of strong men at a time

8. The 'pan' is the steel drum when accomplished as a musical instrument.
9. For detailed discussion of these points see the interview with Selwyn Baptiste published in *Race Today*, 1977, pp.137–42.
10. D. Howe, 'Is a Police Carnival', Race Today, vol.8, no.9, 1976, p.175.

beating the steel in the heart of densely populated London. The impact could not fail to be eloquent, the more so as it almost invariably led to disquiet and complaints by white neighbours, no matter how well-meaning the players were.

The effect of the pan beat on the followers who jumped to the rhythm was electrifying. Like a football team, every band had its supporters who followed its performances during the year and who jumped behind it on carnival days. They supported it financially, physically and morally.

Already, in 1951, a Trinidadian steel band had visited London and played in the Festival of Britain. Some of the players of that band stayed in London for good and did not go back to Trinidad. In 1966, Mrs Laslett invited a West Indian musician, Russell Henderson, to play in the carnival. He recruited two other players and formed a small temporary steel band. A year later, another West Indian musician, Selwyn Baptiste, was asked by Laslett to gather a handful of teenagers and form a band that would play in the carnival. There were only about five youths involved and they took months, hammering their own pans out of oil drums donated by a benefactor. Those two small bands, barely numbering ten people in all, remained the sole steel band players until the end of the 1960s. Then quite suddenly, from about 1973, steel band music became a massive movement.[11]

Along with organising steel bands, Palmer also persuaded enterprising artists to design and make costumes and masques according to Trinidad conventions. One of those artists, who went on to participate in every carnival, winning a prize almost every time, was Laurence Noel, who had been a school teacher since he came to Britain in the early 1960s. He had had nothing to do with Carnival in Trinidad. In 1973, Palmer, who was his friend, asked him to work for the Notting Hill Carnival. His wife urged him to participate and as he himself had felt there was a need to establish a West Indian identity within British society, he accepted the challenge and applied himself to the arts of wire bending to make head masks. He told me that he was sorry not to have started this artistic activity earlier. He ran an art club for West Indian youth called The Trinbago, that had a membership of about two hundred in the 1970s. In the 1973 carnival he joined with the Ebony steel band on the Notting Hill streets and in the following years with other

11. See T. Noel, *The Steelband*, London, the Commonwealth Institute, 1978. For further discussion of steel band music see Chapter 7.

steel bands that had no mas sections of their own. A few weeks before the 1978 Carnival I visited him for a few hours in his house in East London. The entire household, with all the members of his family, were busy making masks for the scores of mas players who had registered for the carnival. Coils of wire, cloth, coloured feathers, steel cutters, finished masks and masks from previous years filled every room and corridor in the house. In the choice of mas themes for Carnival he is guided by the potentialities for colourfulness and exoticism and by costs as well as motif. For the 1977 Notting Hill Carnival his theme was 'Red Indians'; inspired, he explained, by the awe and admiration he felt for the American Indians who had fought so bitterly and valiantly against white domination. He emphasised the educational character of his work, his desire to impart his techniques and art to as many young West Indians as possible. He worked with his family and pupils all year round, not just for the Notting Hill Carnival but for other appearances too: his club had featured in many other festivals and sometimes appeared on television.

Larry Forde was a different type of artist. Sometime Mas Officer of the Carnival Development Committee and head of a mas band called Sukuya, he came to Britain in 1954 when he was 23. He was widely read in mythology, symbolism, costumes, African art generally and African masks in particular. He was a full-time artist. He developed a theme for his mas band after a great deal of thought, then drew the designs for a variety of costumes and masks and subsequently employed art students to cut the cloth and execute the designs. His themes were elaborate and complex; the one for Carnival 1977 – which was the Silver Jubilee year of the coronation of the Queen of England – was 'Mansa Musa's Guest in Regina's Feast', a subtle artistic composition combining African, British and Caribbean elements.

The nature of steel and mas bands' operation in the carnivals could be seen in the development and organisation of Ebony, one of the foremost steel bands in Britain, and first prize winner in successive carnivals. Its founder and musical arranger, known as its Captain, was Randolph Baptiste. He had come from Trinidad in 1968 and soon – he explained to me – was shocked by the discrimination he found, and sought to reestablish his identity as Trinidadian. He started to organise a band and in 1973 was approached by Lesley Palmer who invited him to participate in that year's carnival. With the twenty or so panmen he recruited and trained he did eventually join the carnival, linking with a separate mas band. The next year Ebony established its own mas section.

Ebony's general organiser was, for some time, Hollis Clifton. He had come from Trinidad in 1973, where he had nothing to do with steel bands or Carnival; his middle-class parents had prevented him from joining bands, and anyway at the time he had not himself felt any inclination to join. But when he came to Britain his attitude began to change. His brother-in-law was a member of Ebony and Clifton, being a newcomer, had followed the band as a supporter. Then, he explained to me, he had felt that in order to assert his Trinidad identity he had to become active in the band. 'Here in Britain we need the steel band more than in Trinidad', he argued. He started learning to play the pan and acted as stand-in player to replace absent members. When one member eventually dropped out, Clifton took his place. The band soon discovered his organisational skills and entrusted him with the leading task of organising the mas section. He set up two separate committees, one for the pan section and one for the mas section. In 1978, the two committees were joined into one. He set up five mas sections, in five different neighbourhoods in Greater London, each section having its own local leader. Early in 1978 Clifton visited the different sections and met with local West Indian circles asking for ideas and suggestions regarding the mas theme for the forthcoming carnival. He then presented the various suggestions to the central committee of the band which eventually decided on the specific theme to be adopted, taking into consideration such conventional and constraining factors as costs, weight of masque and colour. Then a trained professional artist drew the sketches and designs. After that an all-night fête was held in a Kensington club when the designs of the various costumes were displayed on the wall so that revellers could decide which costume they would choose. While the band played and slides of previous carnivals were screened in a large adjoining room, people registered orders for the costumes they chose and paid part of the cost.

Further down the hierarchy in the organisation of Ebony, one of the five section leaders was Simon Norbit who came from Trinidad in 1960 and joined Ebony as a supporter in 1973. He did not play pan, preferring dancing and masquerading. He told me: 'Carnival is inside our blood. It is ours and cannot be taken from us. There is nothing degrading about it. Yes, it began in slavery, but that is part of our history'.

Thus the 1971–5 period saw the introduction into the British scene of Trinidad Carnival conventions that had been developed in the course of about 150 years of stormy experience. All their accompanying techniques, arts and symbolism were accommodated and modified to serve the new purposes and interests of a West Indian population that had come mostly from other Caribbean islands with no previous carnival tradition.

3

Youth Rebellion and the Jamaican Connection

The second half of the 1970s witnessed dramatic new developments, both political and cultural, in the structure of the carnival, that were brought about by the sudden appearance on Notting Hill streets of a new generation of West Indian teenagers, born and educated in Britain. It was a generation of alienated, disillusioned, demoralised and rebellious youth, whose plight had deeply affected their parents, souring their sentiments towards and relation with British society.

Many of the teenagers were underachievers in school, who had always trailed behind native British and Asian immigrants from the same schools and localities in their academic achievements. There had been numerous enquiries, research studies and debates about the causes of that failure. Many factors were found to be involved, but the pervading cause was racism in its various manifestations, whether intended or unintended, private or institutional, direct or indirect. Thus a working party of the Black Peoples Progressive Association and Redbridge Community Relations Council, including both teachers and parents, investigated the problem and concluded:

> that the development of a negative self-image in a hostile society was the central cause of West Indian underachievement. British society portrays black people in a negative fashion, and this attitude is internalised by some West Indian children. The resultant poor self-identity, can lead to a lack of confidence and a reduction in motivation which can in turn affect school work.[1]

1. Black Peoples Progressive Association, *et al.* 1978 *Cause for Concern: West Indian Pupils in Redbridge*, Black Peoples Progressive Association and Redbridge Community Council, Ilford, 1978. See also F. Stadlen, 'The Carnival is Over', *Time Higher Educational Supplement*, 1976.

Educational underachievement, racial discrimination and growing scarcity of jobs, produced a vast number of unemployed young blacks. Many of them spent their time hanging around in the streets in neighbourhood gangs. Inevitably, they ran into trouble with the police who invariably suspected them of perpetrating or taking part in criminal offences. Indeed the police were legally allowed by the 'Sus Law' to stop, apprehend and search people they regarded as acting suspiciously. The West Indians tended to keep latenights, usually attending parties or seeking the company of friends in other neighbourhoods until the early hours of the morning, and when they eventually returned home they were intercepted by police patrols. There was hardly any West Indian male who had not been stopped and searched at one time or another.

The youths made their first massive and sudden appearance as an identifiable group in the Notting Hill Carnival in 1975, the tenth anniversary of the festival. Palmer had introduced stationary discos under the A40 fly-over to attract them. A commercial radio station, Capital Radio, which broadcast pop music most of the time and to which most of them used to listen, had become a carnival patron that year, urging its listeners to attend and donating prizes for the best artists. On Carnival Monday, a mobile broadcasting relay unit was placed on a double-decker bus, and the station's disc jockeys went on the air for four hours reporting the developments of the festival as they happened. It was the first year that attendance at the Notting Hill Carnival reached about a quarter of a million people. Inevitably, in such a crowded gathering, there were hundreds of cases of pickpocketing, camera-snatching, illicit sales of alcohol and damage to residential gardens in the area. Only a few policemen were present and they could do little.

At the next carnival, in 1976, over 1,500 policemen were on hand, and, judging by many eyewitness and newspaper reports, they were highhanded and severe.[2] The youths reacted violently. Some of them, loosely organised in gangs, staged lightning attacks, throwing bottles and stones on the police before dispersing rapidly among the crowds to regroup later. Hundreds of policemen and some civilians were injured and taken to hospital.

That confrontation had serious and wide-ranging repercussions. The concern of the present discussion is with its effect on the car-

2. See for example Pilger, 1976, writing for the *Daily Mail*.

nival. It was argued by many of the leaders, and some outside observers, that the youth resorted to violence because they had no means of active artistic participation.[3]

The carnival had, until then, been organised principally by Trinidadians along traditional Trinidad lines. The majority of the West Indian immigrants in Britain were from other Caribbean islands, though, particularly Jamaica, and had no tradition of carnival or steelband music. In Britain the young especially, including the children of Trinidadian parents, had little interest in Trinidad's carnival traditions and conventions. Their 'counter-culture' was expressed and dramatised through the lyrics and rhythm of reggae, and through the concepts, beliefs, symbols and ritual practices of Rastafarianism. There was a tendency for the two cultural forms to be linked, particularly in the songs of Bob Marley and his band, the Wailers.[4]

Reggae songs spoke of violence, blood, fire, police, oppression; but also of love and Jah Rastafari, the black god who would redeem the black people and take them back to the promised land – Africa.[5] Both reggae and rastafarianism developed dramatically during the 1960s in the slums of Kingston, Jamaica, whence they soon spread throughout the rest of the black diaspora. In Britain,

3. See P. Wintour, Bored enough to riot, *New Statesman*, Sept. 1977, pp.291–2.

4. There is a colossal volume of literature on reggae music, principally in popular music journals such as the weekly *Melody Maker*, *Black Echoes* and *New Musical Express*, as well as the monthly *Black Music and Jazz Review*. West Indian journals in Britain publish regular review articles on the latest reggae bands and records. For some discussion of the social and political significance of reggae, see: D. Hebdige, 'Reggae, Rastas and Rudies', in S. Hall and T. Jefferson (eds), *Resistance Through Rituals*, London and Birmingham, Hutchinson, 1975 and *Subculture and the Meaning of Style*, London, Methuen, 1979 and *Cut 'N' Mix*, London, Comedia books, 1987; L.K. Johnson, 'The Reggae Rebellion', *New Society*, 10 June 1976 p.589 and 'Jamaican Rebel Music', *Race and Class*, 1977, pp.397–412; S. Jones, *Black Culture, White Youth*, London, Macmillan Education, 1988; K. Pryce, *Endless Pressure*, Hasmondsworth, Penguin Books, 1979; B. Troyna, 'The Reggae Was', *New Society*, 19 Mar. 1977, pp.491–2. For a more direct discussion of Rastafarianism, see: L.E. Barrett, *Rastafarianism*, London, Heinemann Education, 1977; E. Cashmore, 'The Rastaman Cometh', *New Society*, 1977, pp.382–4 and *The Rastafarian Movement in England*, London, Allen and Unwin, 1979; S. Kitzinges, 'Protest and Mysticism', *J. Sci. Stud. Relig.*, vol. 8, 1969, pp.240–62; R.M. Nettleford, *Mirror, Mirror*, Kingston, William Collins and Sargstes, 1970; M.G. Smith, *et al. The Ras Tafari Movement in Kingston, Jamaica*, Mona, University College of the West Indies, 1960; B. Wilson, *Magic and the Millenium*, London, Paladin, 1973, pp.63–9; J.V. Owens, 'Literature on the Rastafari', *New Community*, 1978, pp. 150–64.

5. Hakim Adi carried out for me a survey of 420 reggae records produced in 1977 and 1978. Of the total, 23 per cent dealt with political issues, 41 per cent with Rastafarianism, 27 per cent with love and 9 per cent with a variety of other topics.

both movements had been embraced by the British-born West Indian youths. Some of the conditions in Jamaica resembled those in the inner cities in Britain, and the new cultural forms could thus be easily transplanted to Britain. However, a British-based reggae soon emerged in the music and songs of such black bands as the Aswads, Cimarons and Steel Pulse, reflecting the black experience in Britain. Because those bands also had to cater to other British audiences, though, their sounds and lyrics were regarded as adulterated, and the youths' attentions remained fixed on Jamaica, from where the latest sounds were eagerly awaited.

Reggae and rastafarianism gave British-born West Indian youths a world view, a political philosophy, an exclusive language, rituals that were manifested in the form of their special appearance and life style and ecstasy achieved through music, dancing and marijuana smoking. More significantly, the two cultural forms became articulating principles for the formation of primary neighbourhood groups which moved in the slums of the inner city to attend one sound system or another.[6]

A sound system is a West Indian disco, operated by one or more men, sometimes from one venue but more often from a number of places. Sound systems vary in their power and the sophistication of their equipment, the collection of records they play and in the originality of their disc jockeys and toasters (artists who against the background of recorded reggae rhythm, improvise songs, poetry and comment on current affairs or convey political messages). A big sound system usually has a core of loyal supporters who follow it wherever it plays and who vote for it in contests with other systems.[7]

Thus for the young West Indians, who formed a large proportion of Britain's West Indian population, reggae was the idiom of cultural and social expression. This fact was not lost on the Trinidad leadership of the carnival, who sought means to accommodate the new music forms. Since the 1975 carnival, sound systems playing reggae records had been installed along the route of the procession, as well as under the fly-over, but the arrangement

6. D. Dodd, 'Police and Thieves on the Streets of Brixton', *New Society*, 1978, pp.598–600; Hebdige, *Subculture* and *Cut 'N' Mix*; Jones, *Black Culture*; M. Phillips, 'Behind the Frontline', *Daily Mirror*, 1 Sept. 1976; M. Stellman, 'Sitting Here in Limbo', *Time Out*, no. 234, 1974, pp.11–13; Troyna, 'Reggae Was'.
7. For a brief discussion of such contests see *New Society*, 23 Mar. 1978, p.655. More details on sound systems can be found in Chapter 6.

proved unsuccessful from the beginning because it split the event between an active, mobile procession and relatively passive, fragmented, stationary, record-playing discos. The young were restless to do something rather than just listen on the spot. The issue became serious in the wake of the 1976 violence.

Two questions arose: whether reggae could blend with steelband music in creating carnival revelry, and whether sound systems could be made mobile. Most carnival leaders and steelband organisers were emphatic that reggae records were not suitable for a mobile carnival for a number of reasons. The steel bands played for long stretches of time, providing the basis of an uninterrupted rhythm for dancing and marching, while reggae records, by contrast, lasted for only a few minutes and so lacked continuity. Revelry involved jumping, and this fitted pan rather than reggae which, some people felt, contained a melancholic element. Further to the pros and cons of the actual musical forms there was the ideological argument that reggae playing sound systems provided 'consumerist' music, rather than the live music, of the steel bands and, moreover, the cultural argument that the musical instruments used in reggae were Western-invented and manufactured, while the pan was West Indian through and through.

There were also technical difficulties. Music for revelry on the road required powerful sounds: steel bands provided this naturally while the sound systems, which also had an emphasis on the power of their sound, provided it by use of strong amplifiers; many of the hundreds of sound systems operating in West Indian neighbourhoods in Greater London at that time boasted of having as much as 1,000-watt amplifiers. For the sound systems it was also difficult to provide mobile music because movement disturbed the needle on the record. This though proved to be the easiest of the technical problems to resolve through using cassettes instead of records.

In the following years there was great progress towards resolving some of those artistic and technical problems. In the first place, there were sustained efforts to accommodate steelband and reggae music the tastes of the West Indian population generally. Young people were being educated in steelband music and many schools with large numbers of West Indian children developed their own steel bands. In parties organised by the carnival committees for the young, steel band and calypso regularly alternated with reggae. The BBC daily radio programme 'Black Londoners', under the cultural direction of West Indians, provided both kinds of music.

Since the 1970s there had also been a tendency for some reggae bands to include among their instruments one or two pans; on the other hand, some steel bands employed one or more of the more conventional musical instruments. In all pre-carnival dances, fêtes, launching parties, gala performances and afternoon parties for children, both types of music were played. Some ingenious devices were also developed to make the record-playing sound systems more like live music and more adaptable to local conditions in their tunes and lyrics. West Indian sound systems in Britain employed expensive, highly elaborate electronic equipment that enabled the operators to intervene with the recorded sound, raising the level of some sound elements and lowering others. More significantly, in addition to the disc jockey, many systems employed a toaster whose function resembled that of the traditional Trinidad calypso accompaniment of the steel band. Finally, elaborate devices increasingly overcame the technical problems of putting sound systems on mobile platforms and providing enough battery power to produce loud sounds. Thus, from the 1976 carnival onwards a steadily increasing number of mobile sound systems appeared on the streets of Notting Hill, followed by groups of masqueraders and dancers.

As an index to those developments in the cultural forms and politics of the Notting Hill Carnival, I turn to a brief account of a small mas band called Lion Youth. The group was first organised in 1977 by two young women, Leslie and Betty, one from Jamaica and the other from Guyana. Both women were graduates of an arts college in North London; both had operated behind the scenes in previous carnivals as costume designers, working anonymously for leading carnival men.

Early in 1977 they decided to form their own mas band. They resented the fact that the carnival was dominated by males, when, they argued, most of the preparation and work were done by females. Indeed, one of them said that women were the pillars of the whole West Indian community in Britain. They also resented the domination of carnival by Trinidadians, when the majority of British West Indians were from other islands. Both of them were in close contact with black teenagers and so were well aware of the problems, thoughts and sentiments of the new British-born generation. They wanted to capture the mood of the youths and so chose for their first masquerading theme 'Rastafarian Representations'. One of the women explained to me that she herself had always been interested in African messianic movements and was full of awe and admiration for the Lenshina prophetic movement.[8]

The women approached the church of a section of the Rastafarian movement known as the 'Twelve Tribes of Israel' for support. Church members responded favourably and provided the group with space for a workshop and with food during the weeks of preparation. Leslie and Betty also elicited financial support from a variety of sources: the black bookshop New Beacon, the mas band Sukuya, the Carnival Development Committee and the Race Today Collective. Twenty-five girls and two boys appeared in the masquerade in colourful procession, the girls wearing costumes in gold, red and green (a combination representing both the Ethiopian flag and the colours of the Rastafarian movement). They carried umbrellas displaying the Lion of Judah and the Star of David, and a banner commemorating Marcus Garvey, regarded as the galvanising spirit of the black liberation movement of the 1920s and 1930s and in effect the founder of Rastafarianism.[9]

Lion Youth's appearance in the 1977 carnival was acclaimed as a significant success. One of the two leaders, Betty, returned to the West Indies immediately afterward, but Leslie worked energetically for a whole year to organise a bigger mas band for the next carnival. About ninety girls and boys, aged between 15 and 18 registered to take part. The theme chosen was 'Yut War'. In view of the group's success in the previous year, the Arts Council gave the band a grant of £900 for the preparations. About fifty local West Indian men and women, many of them parents of the participating youths, helped. Leslie contacted a well-known sound system called Peoples War, run by two brothers, to provide reggae music for the street procession on Carnival Monday. Half of the Arts Council grant was spent on equipment to render the sound system mobile. The mas players paid £8 each for their costumes. The leader of the group aimed to involve as many people as possible in the preparations for the carnival, and hoped to establish her band as a framework for training the young, teaching them to make their own costumes and masks, decide on their own themes, provide their own music and develop their own consciousness of the problems affecting the lives of the West Indians.

8. For an account of the Lenshina movement see R. Rotberg 'The Lenshina Movement of Northern Rhodesia', *Rhodes-Livingst. J.*, no. 29, 1961.

9. For further details about this band see *Race Today*, 1977, p.143.

The story of Lion Youth indicates that a new generation of British-born youths appeared on the streets of Notting Hill during the 1976–80 period to participate in the carnival and to develop new themes and new artistic forms, and thereby change the structure of the event. In this way the London carnival was continuously transformed, within certain cultural and social conventions, into an expression of, and an instrument for, the development of a new homogeneous West Indian culture that transcended affiliations to islands of origin, to confront the economic and political realities of contemporary Britain.

Between them, Lion Youth and a few other, similar bands accommodated only a small proportion of West Indian youths. The majority were little involved in the central cultural activities of the carnival. In the meantime, serious public debate about the problems of the carnival continued. Already, in reaction to the 1975 carnival there was mounting opposition to the continuation of the event raised by a strong body of residents who officially petitioned the authorities in their hundreds, complaining of the deafening noise, of the ruin of their gardens, used as lavatories or as a nest for sexual intercourse. They were supported in their complaints by the local council who pointed out that the carnival had become national in scale and that it was unfair that the locality should bear the brunt of the burden. The deputy leader of the Kensington and Chelsea Council, Alderman Methuen, sent a letter to the Home Secretary (then Roy Jenkins) telling him he expected a great deal of trouble if the carnival was staged in 1976, suggesting it should be cancelled and stating that the Home Secretary was the only authority empowered to do this. A spokesman from the Home Office said that that was nonsense, as the Council itself had the authority to stop the carnival. The demand that the carnival should be stopped has been continuously raised in various quarters through the years, but the carnival makers have remained adamant. The carnival leaders have declared their inalienable right to stage it, pointing out that its problems are no different from those of other crowd events, such as football matches.

The suggestion of other opponents of the carnival that it should be moved from Notting Hill to a nearby stadium or public park was also vehemently rejected by the carnival leaders. They argued that as an essentially mobile spectacle, the character of the carnival would be altogether changed if it was confined within a narrow space.

A more serious attempt on the part of the authorities to ease the situation in Notting Hill took the form of encouraging the development of a number of mini-carnivals in other areas of Greater London where significant numbers of West Indians lived – such as Brixton, Brent and Finsbury Park. Mini-carnivals had already been organised by West Indians in other towns and cities – Reading, Leeds, Bristol, for instance – but were held on other days in order to enable people to travel to participate in the Notting Hill event.

Almost all the efforts ended in failure. In assessing the reasons for this failure, it would perhaps be more instructive to examine, not the cases of failure, but one of 'success': the Finsbury Park Carnival, which was staged regularly on the same day as the Notting Hill Carnival from August 1978 to August 1981.

The initiative to hold a carnival in Finsbury Park was taken by a clergyman, Pastor Ruport Morris, who was born in Jamaica, where he had been trained as an Evangelist missionary, before immigrating to Britain. Among his many accomplishments in his new country, was founding the Ruport Morris Welfare and Advice Centre, which incorporated a 'Walk-in Counselling Youth Club' that provided a service for youths who were homeless, disturbed, in trouble with the law or socially deprived and for adults with legal and welfare problems – to paraphrase his personal visiting card. In comments on violence in the Notting Hill Carnival he had stated scathingly that West Indian youths were not interested in 'Tin-pan Calypso' and that the carnival was no good because it had not offered an active role for the young. He consequently proposed the staging of a new carnival in the Finsbury Park area to draw the youth away from the troubles of the Notting Hill event.

A number of sympathetic West Indian men living in the area expressed support. Among them was Sam Dowridge, who had come from Trinidad to Britain in 1962. He had regularly and actively participated in the Notting Hill Carnival but was shocked, and even burst into tears, when the violence broke out in the 1976 Carnival. He told me later that the event was a turning point in his thinking about Carnival. Then he was approached by Pastor Morris who asked him to join hands with him and others to organise a local carnival. He immediately thought that his commitment to the welfare of the young obliged him to cooperate. Indeed, he had earlier decided to sell his electric appliances business and return to

41

Trinidad, taking his family with him, but now felt it was his moral duty to stay on and do his utmost to help. A few weeks before the 1978 carnival I visited him at his home in Leyton Station. He acted not only as a member of the Carnival Committee but also as the leader of a masquerading band. His house was alive with feverish activity, as his wife, daughter and others worked with him preparing the costumes and masks for his team, which was to enact the Legend of Robin Hood. His elder daughter was going to appear as Queen of the Band, and an elaborate mobile throne and a crown were being made for her. Costumes for fifty mas players were also in the making. He was tense and anxious in case his band should turn out to be a flop. He said he did not like politics in Carnival and was very frank in stating that the aim of the local carnival was to attract some of the youths away from the Notting Hill event.

Early in 1978 the Finsbury Park Westindian Carnival Committee was set up, with Pastor Morris serving as Organising Secretary. Three high ranking police officers who participated in the meetings were described as consultants. Financial support was given by the three borough councils involved: Islington, Hackney and Haringey. Further support was provided by the Arts Council and by the Commission for Racial Equality. As Carnival Monday approached, 5,000 posters announcing the event in Finsbury Park were distributed. Also, the first number of *Finsbury Park Westindian Carnival Souvenir Magazine* was published by the Committee, featuring a preface by Pastor Morris and reproducing greeting messages from the mayors of Islington, Hackney and Haringey. In his introductory remarks Pastor Morris noted that the Notting Hill Carnival was 'bereft of activities and attractions for the young people, who finally got bored and frustrated and were driven to unrest, unpleasantness and confrontation of a frightening nature'. His implication was that his carnival would help to resolve those problems.

When Carnival Monday – 28 August 1978 – came, there was, indeed, tranquillity and calm in the Finsbury Park Carnival, but the youths and the tens of thousands of West Indians living in the area were not there. They had shied away from 'their' carnival and travelled a long way to take part in the Notting Hill event, where, by then, the customary ritual of youths rioting and behaving with violence towards the end of the day, was staged without fail. The main grassroots participators in Finsbury Park were Rupert Morris' church congregation and the youths affiliated to his club, all of

42

whom were under pressure to attend. The rest of the local West Indians followed the calls of a different type of organisation and leadership.

Finsbury Park was a highly volatile community with scores of associations of different sorts, among them The Black Parents Movement and the Black Youth Movement, with highly educated, essentially middle-class, leadership. The masses of young people were kept informally informed and advised by the artists and organisers of the local sound systems. (The Finsbury Park area was described by the local West Indians as 'Soundsystemland'.)

Prominent among the local young leaders were two brothers, Keith and Michael La Rose. Their father was John La Rose, an eminent West Indian writer, publisher and political activist. In 1964 he founded the New Beacon Bookshop in Stroud Green Road near Finsbury Park Station. In fact it was more than a bookshop, serving also as a publishing company and a distribution centre for literary sources for teachers and colleges concerned with multicultural education and for books and information about Africa and the Caribbean. It also provided an address for a number of associations. The New Beacon was, indeed, a centre for the local intellectuals and a focus for community consciousness. Similar bookshops with the same characteristics providing similar services operated in all the major West Indian neighbourhoods in different parts of London, and, probably because of their cultural and political significance, they had been the targets of frequent attacks by racist arsonists. In 1977, seven of the bookshops combined to form 'The Bookshop Joint Action', which petitioned government authorities, complaining of police inaction in preventing or investigating such attacks.

The two La Rose brothers took it in turn to work with their father at the New Beacon Bookshop on a part-time basis. For the rest of their time they operated their sound system, called Peoples War, which had a large following among the youths of the Finsbury Park area. Their influence on the youths must have been great. At the same time they were closely involved with and active on the Notting Hill Carnival Committee (CDC), of which Michael La Rose at one time acted as vice-chairman.

On 8 August 1978, only three weeks before Carnival Monday, the Black Youth Movement in the Finsbury Park area distributed a leaflet entitled: *It's a Police Carnival – Don't go to the Finsbury Park West Indian Carnival.* It declared: 'The Black Youth

Movement call on all black youth of North London, not to go to the Pastor Morris' Finsbury Park Carnival. This event is aimed at getting as many black youths as possible away from the Notting Hill Carnival'. It went on to say that Rupert Morris had received enormous amounts of money with which he was trying to buy the services of masquerade bands, steel bands and sound systems. It warned the youth that in Finsbury Park the police would have no trouble in surrounding the carnival and 'there will be no escape'. The statement continued:

> The BYM support the Notting Hill Carnival organised by the Carnival Development Committee (CDC). It is the only major cultural festival in Britain run and organised by black people. We call on black youth and all sections of the black community to attend and participate in Carnival at Notting Hill. . . . The Finsbury Park Carnival is yet another attempt to divide and defeat what we as black people have built up over the past 13 years. The BYM will be participating in Carnival as Lion Youth playing 'Yut War', Race Today Renegades playing 'Forces of Victory' and Peoples War Sound System. At the Notting Hill Carnival we will have the freedom of the streets, not a fenced enclosure surrounded by police.

The statement was signed by the Black Youth Movement. The Finsbury Carnival was duly held. It was attended by white and black dignitaries who, together with the disabled, were seated on chairs. Also in attendance were many local women with their small children.

The mini carnival survived in that uncertain composition for four years. Like the Notting Hill event, it was attended by a large police force. *The Times* in comment on the 1981 Finsbury Park Carnival said: 'Rarely can so massive a police presence . . . have supervised so little'.[10] After that the Finsbury Park Carnival ceased to exist.

---

10. *The Times,* 1 Sept. 1981.

4

The Carnival is Contested

The 1980s were ushered in by the rise of Thatcherism, by a dramatic acceleration in the rate of unemployment and violent black youth rioting in the main cities of England. On the cultural front, the deaths of the musician Bob Marley and Ethiopian Emperor Haile-Selassie, who had been deified by the Rastafarians, marked the slow waning of the significance of Rastafarianism. This itself led, in particular, to the abandonment of the principle of return to Africa, as more West Indians settled down to operate within the British system. They struggled against racism through such tactics as massive organised marches and in increasing participation in the electoral process in local politics. On the carnival front, different state apparatuses were used to contest and contain the celebration, but it continued to be a tense event, with violence ever lurking just below the surface. The period of 1980 to 1986 saw the structural integration of the mobile bands and the stationary sound systems, and the rise of the stall holders as effective agents of cultural homogenisation.

When it became evident that the Notting Hill Carnival could not be banned or geographically dispersed in mini carnivals, the authorities sought to contest it and contain it – economically, politically, culturally and ideologically. Different strategies were set in motion to achieve that, with subtle, loose coordination of policy by different public authorities: the Home Office, the police, the Council for Racial Equality, the local council, the now defunct Greater London Council and the Arts Council.

Towards the middle of 1981 a turning point was reached when, as a result of behind-the-scenes discussions, a moderate, unified organising committee, the Carnival and Arts Committee (CAC), was elected. Its existance had been brought about principally by the decision of the Arts Council earlier in the year to ignore the two rival carnival committees then existing, the CDC and the CAC, and to deal directly with the bands about funding.

In the early years the Arts Council had been cagey about giving financial support to the Notting Hill Carnival on the grounds that it was not an artistic event. For an institution which principally allocated money to such elitist arts as the opera and the theatre it was difficult to see any artistic merit in popular masquerades and in 'repetitive jerky jumping that went on all day', as one Council official put it. Thus considerable polemic had gone on between the carnival organisers and officials of the Arts Council over whether carnival arts were truly artistic. Darcus Howe, chairman of the Carnival Development Committee from 1976 to 1981, retorted in 1978 in front of journalists:' Our artists are not Picassoes. . . . They are not reviewed in *The Times* or the *Guardian*. . . . They are nevertheless artists in their own right. . . . Our art is as valid and as important as any other'.[1]

After a great deal of pressure the Council reluctantly had agreed to give a certain amount of funding to the organising committees, who duly distributed some of the money among the bands. There were bitter quarrels and complaints among the organisers and the bands, and demands for public accountability to show where the money was going. In the process, the steel bands and mas bands had to declare publicly to which of the two committees each gave its loyalty. The difficulties came to a head in 1981 and the Arts Council declared that it would no longer give the funds to the organising committees but that the bands should apply directly to it for financial assistance. It was agreed that the artistic merit of the bands would be assessed by the criteria of Caribbean aesthetic norms and artistic conventions. The officer in charge of the Arts Community Budget at the time was asked to oversee the procedure. She was well acquainted with the Notting Hill Carnival and had visited the Caribbean at carnival times. She had done her utmost to convince the directors of the Arts Council that they had misunderstood and undervalued carnival arts, which were indeed of significant aesthetic merit.

A panel of five Afro-Caribbean men and women, chosen for their long standing experience of and association with carnivals, was set up. The panel interviewed representatives of all mas bands

1. From my personal notes of the proceedings of a seminar held by the CDC at the Commonwealth Institute in 1978.

applying for funds. Each band was asked about its proposed masquerade theme, the meaning of that theme, the procedure adopted in choosing it, the extent of the involvement of the ordinary band members in its choice and the timetable of the mas camp, the steel band, or any other type of music that would accompany the group on the day of the carnival. The panel then decided which band would be funded and to what extent.

To assist the bands to obtain more funds, the Arts Council organised a promotional party intended to persuade businesses, black and white, to sponsor individual bands who would, for example wear T-shirts advertising the sponsor, as was the practice in Trinidad. Two steel bands and a sound system played at the party, and a variety of Caribbean foods and drinks were served. An Arts Council Chief gave the opening speech in which he stressed the importance of carnival in developing a multicultural Britain. The promotion was a success and many black firms were convinced for the first time that the carnival had become an 'officially' institutionalised, secure affair, and that it was worth their while sponsoring it.

The new policy and procedure enforced by the Arts Council had far-reaching internal political and cultural consequences. The two old committees virtually lost their control over the bands and, in view of their past bickering and of their failure to submit publicly accurate accounts, they became discredited. There was sustained pressure both from inside the carnival movement and from outside it, to set up a new unified committee. A public meeting was arranged on 7 May 1981 and the new committee, the CAC, was elected. The political activists from the two old committees were not elected. A respectable celebrity, Mr Oswald Gibbs, a former High Commissioner for Granada in London, was invited to become chairman of the committee. He accepted and duly instituted round table discussions. Representatives of the mas bands and steel bands were co-opted onto the committee and took part in continuous consultations. In a Chairman's Introduction to the *Notting Hill Carnival 1982* annual magazine, Gibbs pointed out that funds and support were given by the Arts Recreation Committee of the Greater London Council, that the Home Office had given approval to the Commission for Racial Equality for financial assistance and that German Lager importers had sponsored the carnival in a major promotion of their Dortmunder 'Kronen Classic' Beer.

The new committee soon gained the respect and trust of the relevant public institutions, indeed of the Establishment generally. In subsequent years the annual glossy magazine of the Carnival published in its first few pages photocopies of letters of praise and good wishes for the carnival from important officials and dignitaries: Caribbean High Commissioners; Scotland Yard chiefs; the Archbishop of Westminster; the Chairman of the Commission for Racial Equality; the Mayor of the Royal Borough of Kensington and Chelsea; the Prime Minister; the Leader of the Labour Party, the Leader of the Liberal Party; the Leader of the Greater London Council; the Arts Council; the Commissioner of Police of the Metropolis; Prince Charles, the Prince of Wales and the mayors of a number of London boroughs in which large numbers of West Indians lived. Some of the organisers and artists were invited to parties in Buckingham Palace.

The churches played their own part in steering the carnival along the right path. On the eve of Carnival Sunday a Thanks-giving Service was celebrated in Westminster Cathedral, at which a steel band played. Many church leaders visited the area on Carnival Monday and a few took part in the dancing. Even white nuns joined in the activity.

On 12 May 1983, the first ever permanent office for the CAC was ceremoniously inaugurated in the presence of the Mayor and the Mayoress of the Royal Borough of Kensington and Chelsea; representatives from the High Commissions of Trinidad and Tobago, Guyana, Grenada and Jamaica; the press and members of the local community. Also, the first full-time, salaried CAC administrator was appointed.

In 1984 Oswald Gibbs left the chairmanship of the committee to return to the diplomatic corps as Grenada's High Commissioner to the United Kingdom. He was succeeded by Alex Pascall, a professional journalist, broadcaster, disc jockey, master of ceremonies and musician, who injected further excitement and colour, as well as respect, into the carnival. He had a wide reputation both within and without the West Indian community in both Britain and the Caribbean.

The 1980s also saw the launching of the Carnival Industrial Project conducted under the Youth Training Scheme of the Manpower Services Commission. Its manager for some time was Victor Crichlow, a long time carnival leader, treasurer of the new Carnival and Arts Committee. Instruction and guidance were given enthusiastically by dedicated carnivalists who were intent on passing on to the young the conventional carnival skills and forms. Whenever and wherever possible the skills and techniques taught were transferable, so that the graduates would qualify for employment in skilled jobs in the industrial sector generally. The management committee was inundated with applications, and the waiting list was considerable. About thirty youths at a time were taken on and trained in leathercraft, silk-screen printing, steel pan making, wire-bending and costume making. Standards in some of the sections were so high that it was claimed that, in steel pan making, for example, orders were received even from Trinidad and Tobago, the birthplace of the instrument. The project was supported by organisations such as Grassroots, Caribbean Cultural International, Unity Association, Black People's Information Centre and the Acklam Play Centre.[2]

While committed to keep the carnival distinctly West Indian in cultural forms, conventions and leadership, the CAC was conscious of the potential for attracting white onlookers and revellers. Indeed, carnival leaders had for long been claiming that 'the greatest street cultural event in Europe' had been attracting large numbers of tourists from Europe and elsewhere who spent a great deal of money, to the benefit of the country, and that it would be only fair to give some of the revenue gained nationally to finance and further develop the carnival. In order to convince the authorities about the validity of those claims, in 1988 the CAC commissioned the Harris Research Survey to assess the amount of wealth that the carnival was creating for the country.

It was, of course, obvious that vast numbers of white Britons thronged to Notting Hill Carnival every year, drinking, dancing and eating traditional Caribbean foods, buying handicrafts and art objects. Indeed, Alex Pascall, in one of his expansive enthusiastic moments said in public that it was his dream and practical endeavour to develop the carnival into a British cultural event; although, on many other occasions, he had been categorical that carnival was uniquely West Indian: 'Carnival is our heritage, our cultural identity without which our children would not know who we are!' The dominant sentiment of many West Indian carnivalists in this respect was *pride* in demonstrating to white Britons their cultural achievements, their important contribution to British multicultural society.

Processes were therefore set in motion to institutionalise the

2. See the *Notting Hill Carnival* 1984 magazine.

London Carnival, to integrate it with the major institutions of British society, and thereby to contain it and to some extent control it. Such control was inevitably limited, though. The CAC, moderate, professional and cooperative though it was, had no direct control over the masses who attended the carnival. The committee cooperated with the police in fixing the route of the parade and the sites where the live rock bands would perform; it appointed stewards to accompany the mobile bands, to ensure that they would follow the prescribed route in an orderly manner, and cooperated with the local council about the installation of temporary toilets and the procedure for cleaning up when the carnival was over. It registered the various participating bands, appointed panels of judges for the competitions for prizes, allocated money for those prizes and raised money from various institutions to finance the administration and the competitions. It registered and collected fees from the hundreds of carnival stall holders selling food, drinks and a wide variety of other goods, and allocated places for them. It also registered the sound systems and allocated their positions. Finally, it published the annual glossy colour magazine, providing information about the bands and about the activities of the committee, photographs of previous carnivals, as well as the results of the competitions in the last year's carnival, and sought to educate the public about the carnival and its significance.

Indirectly, the committee exercised what must have been a great deal of moral pressure on a wide range of people, through the extensive, overlapping social networks linking its members with the various members and followers of masquerading bands, steel bands, sound systems, clubs, island associations, calypsonians (singers, composers and players of calypso), costume designers and makers. All those people would no doubt mobilise their relatives, friends, followers and associates, as support for the carnival enterprise. These overlapping networks of social relations must have been of immense importance in the exercise of control over many carnivalists, if only because the many thousands of people actively involved in the carnival had developed a vested interest in an orderly, peaceful, successful celebration. Through their spokesmen the committee also appealed directly to the police in community papers and on the radio, speaking particularly to the youth, beseeching them not to spoil the enterprise, pointing out that 'the Carnival is our heritage, our identity', and that any trouble they caused might prompt the authorities to stop it forthright.

50

But all those kinds of pressure and means of control had only limited possibilities and their effectiveness was unpredictable and unreliable. The masses of youths, who had been demographically growing in number, had generally become more embittered, militant and violent than ever before. During the greater part of the 1980s the number of unemployed in Britain generally trebled, and, under the Conservative government led my Margaret Thatcher, the divide between rich and poor grew dramatically deeper. Black youth fared worst, with a rate of unemployment many times that of white youth. Although the notorious 'Sus' Law was repealed, new laws were enacted that enabled the police to continue their 'stop and search' policy. Racism continued unabated in every walk of life. Research by a team of psychiatrists in London found that black people born in Britain to West Indian parents were three times more likely to be taken to hospital and diagnosed as schizophrenic as were other black immigrants, and twelve times more likely to be than were white Britons.[3] A psychiatrist commented: 'It is a question of racism. . . . Black people are being driven psychotic by our society'.

Early in the 1980s, thousands of black youths had burst out in massive violence and fought pitched battles with the police, using bricks, bottles, iron bars, petrol bombs, setting on fire buildings and vehicles, smashing shops and looting their contents. The fiercest battle raged for three days in April 1981 in Brixton (London), where a large number of West Indians (most originally from Jamaica) lived. The result was 242 casualties and 168 arrests.[4]

An American-style 'hot summer' was predicted for that year and many people, both white and black, police and civilian, expected a similar flare up in Notting Hill, almost certainly during the forthcoming 1981 carnival over the August Bank Holiday. Tension mounted as the date approached, with rumours that black youth and the police had been preparing for a violent showdown. The extreme right-wing party, the National Front, planned a march nearby to take place on Carnival Sunday and threatened to attack the carnival if the authorities did not cancel it.

The carnival, however, was duly held, with 13,000 policemen attending – the largest force ever to have been deployed for the carnival. The expected riot did not occur. The National Front

3. See the *Guardian*, 30 Sept. 1987.
4. *The Times*, 13 Apr. 1981. See also 'The night Brixton burnt' *The Observer*, 16 Apr. 1981 and 'The bloody battle of Brixton', *The Sunday Times*, 25 Apr. 1982.

march had been banned, though about three hundred members of that party held a rally in Fulham, two miles away. They were challenged by a group of about one hundred Anti-Nazi League members; the police kept the two groups apart. The National Front made no attempt to go to Notting Hill to disturb the carnival, and apart from normal minor incidents, the two days of carnival passed peacefully. Because of the tension and rumours, fewer white people had attended than in previous years.

Anticipated rioting in Notting Hill again loomed large a few months later, though, on 20 April 1982. Tension had continued in the area between the police and black youths since the 1981 carnival. Small daily confrontations had occurred in which jeers and insults were exchanged. On Christmas eve 1981 the police had once again raided the Mangrove restaurant with violence and arrests. This itself followed another confrontation that had occurred two weeks earlier when the police had withdrawn after their vans had been attacked during a drug arrest.

The flashpoint for the violence in April came when a black couple were stopped and searched by three uniformed police officers. Soon an angry gathering crowd forcibly freed the couple. The police withdrew and called for help. Police cars were subsequently stoned, including that of the local police commander, and barricades were hastily erected in All Saints Road. Within minutes over a hundred policemen from the new frontline, immediate response units, appeared on the scene, the men wearing black, flame-resistant overalls and armed with truncheons and protective shields. They launched an attack and stormed the Mangrove, where about forty men and women were present, allegedly hitting people and destroying property. With lightning speed they cleared the barricades, seized petrol bombs and made twenty-four arrests, employing new strategies and tactics that had been developed in the light of experience from the riots of Bristol, Liverpool, Manchester and Brixton.

The local black community was bitter about what had happened, particularly that the personal identification numbers of the riot police had been hidden under their new overalls, making it impossible to lodge complaints against any particular policeman. Frank Crichlow, whose Mangrove club was extensively damaged by the raid, said the police used the search for drugs as an excuse to terrorise the local community.[5]

5. For details on these events see the *Guardian,* 22 Apr. 1982; *The Times,* 22 Apr. 1982; *The Sunday Times,* 25 Apr. 1982; *The Kensington Post,* 23 and 30 Apr. 1982.

The black youths who had staged the riots in the various areas of Britain, together with many others, were conceivably the young revellers in Notting Hill during the two-day carnival. Only a fraction of them took part in organised masquerading bands. The overwhelming majority milled around, restlessly moving from one side to the other, often in gangs of varying sizes, looking for excitement, deriving confidence and strength from being part of a much bigger force of black youth. Exploiting the anonymity of being in a crowd, some of them engaged in pickpocketing, bag snatching and other petty crimes. When they gathered in large numbers in one place they formed a formidable force which could potentially be easily and rapidly mobilised for more concerted and serious collective acts of violence, thus transforming individual behaviour into a political confrontation. The authorities were unwilling to take the chance of this happening and regularly provided massive policing for the carnival, drafting to the Notting Hill area between 7,000 and 9,000 men and women who were highly corporately organised, linked by intricate inter-personnel systems and car, and helicopter radio and video contacts, with cameras positioned at different points, all relaying visual and sound information to a central headquarters, especially set up for the occasion (described by *The Independent* as being Battle-of Britain-like) and manned by high ranking officers and assistants.

The youths did take part in sporadic, expressive 'cultural' performances. They focused on the stationary sound systems, moving in the course of the day from one to another. Indeed, nearly all their culture and ideology had been shaped around the sound systems: they were the main supporters of the sounds, and the sounds catered for them and thrived on their support.

The controversy that had risen during the late 1970s about the role of reggae music in the cultural structure of the carnival developed in the course of the 1980s into a full blown clash of musics and organisational strategies. At times the worst fears of the traditional carnivalists, of a sharp split of the event between the mobile masquerading bands and the powerful sound systems, were realised. Fundamentally, however, the carnival had become an integrated whole in terms of personnel, as the crowds around the sound systems were always on the move. It was, in fact, the mobility of the sound systems crowds that made policing the event an exacting and costly task.

Over the years, the number of mobile masquerading bands steadily increased, reaching about fifty a year in the late 1980s. The number of people actively involved in them, together with their followers, formed only a relatively small proportion of the hundreds of thousands who attended the carnival, however. The Carnival and Art Committee had been so concerned about the low participation in the mas bands that they adopted as the slogan for the 1987 carnival 'Don't come to Carnival to *watch* Mas; come to Carnival to *play* Mas'.

The sound systems were arenas of social interaction and cultural integration. Symbolically, they were more significant than the mas bands, though newspapers and the media in general inevitably represented the carnival by pictures of exotic and colourful costumes of the mas bands. West Indians from the different islands were exposed to each others' foods and styles. Trinidadians ate Jamaican fried dumpling, ackee and saltfish and Jamaicans ate Trinidadian roti, crab and callallo. There was a great deal of cultural homogenisation, and men and women who lived in different parts of London and the provinces interacted with one another and formed new friendships or revived earlier ones. Different forms of music were played: soca, calypso, soul, reggae. And there was a great deal of toasting commenting on different aspects of the life of black people in Britain. The sound of music pouring out of the many large and powerful speakers that were positioned in different places around the amplifiers was deafening and intoxicating, and the thud of the beat shook the audiences down to their bones. Many were almost oblivious to the mas bands that passed by. This caused tension between the mas bands and the sound systems.

The organisers appealed to the sound system operators to lower the volume of their music when a mas band passed, pointing out the great efforts and creativity invested in mounting the masquerades. All to no avail. One year I watched the BBC radio team who were covering the carnival live on Radio London move their vans and equipment several times in a desperate attempt to find a quieter spot, but without much success.

Under pressure from the organising committee, in 1986 the major sound systems formed The British Association of Sound Systems, which came to be represented by two delegates on the management committee of the CAC. The Association introduced rules of conduct for its members and allocated sites for them. It was hoped that the problem would be solved, but many systems did not register with the Association and did not heed its rules, and the issue has remained alive all the time.

The crucial factor in this cleavage between the mobile mas bands and the stationary sound systems was not reggae music as such, which actually only a few of the sound systems tended to play. In fact reggae music generally dwindled in its popularity and political significance during the 1980s. For one thing Bob Marley, who had popularised it and raised it to an international level, died in 1981. Its decline also went hand in hand with the decline of Rastafarianism, the cult that had inspired it during the 1970s and whose deity, Haile Selassie, had died a few years earlier. More importantly, black political activists in Britain regularly attacked the cult's myth of 'the return to Africa' as a defeatist ideology and urged the youth to organise for effective political action against racism, emphasising that 'We are here to stay'. In fact, an increasing number of sound systems played mainly soca, instead of reggae in carnival – a loud, fast and cheerful music that combined elements from soul, calypso, and reggae, within a conventional upbeat.

Neither was the technical problem of rendering the sound systems mobile the crucial factor in the split. Indeed, as the years went by, more sound systems came to be operated by adequate battery power, were mounted on trucks and played for some of the increasing number of masquerading bands.

The ideal music for the 'jump up' in the mobile mas bands continued to be that of steel bands. The 1980s saw dramatic developments in the steelband movement in Britain. In 1982 the leading steel bands of the metropolis formed The London Brotherhood of Steel, which eventually represented twelve bands, among them: Ebony, London All Stars, Mangrove, Metronomes and Glissando. The chairman was Randolph Baptiste, a veteran steelband leader originally from Trinidad. Its office was at the Tabernacle Community Association. Scores of school-based steel bands, also evolved as part of the curriculum for multicultural education, most of them affiliated to the British Association of Steelbands, under the chairmanship of Terry Noel. Hand in hand with these developments in steelband music, and as part of it, there was a rise and rapid development of an original British-based calypso movement, for which a separate association was formed. From the spring of 1983 an annual day-long festival of steelband concerts and competitions was held at the Royal Festival Hall, which was usually the venue for concerts by leading national and international orchestras. The festival was financially supported by the (now defunct) Greater

London Council (GLC), which was controlled at the time by the Labour Party and headed by the radical left-wing councillor, Ken Livingstone.

But the steel bands were expensive to hire and highly problematic to operate. Sound systems, on the other hand, were cheaper to hire and easier to handle, and there were in any case masquerading bands whose members preferred them.

Nor were inter-island rivalries the cause of the split. Some traditional carnival makers who had come originally from Trinidad, had at one time bitterly attacked the sound systems for bringing in troublesome offspring of Jamaican parents to spoil their carnival, and had thus injected into the polemic an old tension between Trinidad and Jamaica over the leadership of a proposed Caribbean federation. That, however, was a dead issue without consequence for the new alignments in Britain. The children of Trinidadian descent joined others in congregating around the sound systems, and children of once Jamaican parents joined masquerading bands that were accompanied by steel bands.

The sound systems catered principally for the young generation, the overwhelming majority of whom did not join the mobile masquerading bands because they did not want to be trapped by 'the system'. Joining a masquerading band would restrict their freedom of action. It would require them to register with a band, attend its preparatory meetings, and, more importantly, to stick with it throughout the duration of the carnival, moving slowly along a route prescribed by the police, wearing masquerading costumes that could be easily identified amid largely non-masquerading crowds; they would be obliged, moreover, to keep in a fixed position within the band in accordance with the theatrical theme and to associate with the same members of the band. Furthermore, bands on the road were generally under some restrictions imposed by the funding bodies, who were usually government institutions or commercial firms and that would entail the existence of a responsible leadership within the band who would exercise their authority over members. Bands also had to register with the Carnival Committee which would appoint stewards to maintain discipline around it when the band moved and mobile mas bands were accompanied by a number of policemen who would march with them.

By not joining a masquerading band on the other hand, the

youths would avail themselves of a variety of 'sounds' by moving from one sound system to another; would be able to dance, smoke marijuana, eat and talk where and when they liked. They would be in the company of their usual gang, cooperating with one another, defending one another and entertaining one another. Above all, if they were free from the discipline and visibility of the mas bands, the carnival offered them the unique opportunity of the year: to outwit, outmanoeuvre, confront and attack their arch enemy – the police, who in the light of their past experience objectified for them a racist and oppressive social system. On ordinary days they could be easily detected and singled out, being black in a sea of whites, in the carnival they would fade into anonymity within a sea of blacks.

The carnival leadership was fully aware of all of this, and had consistently asked the police not to provoke the youths by being present in large numbers. Two young members of the CAC wrote in the magazine *Notting Hill Carnival 1981*

> We as youth cannot really begin to enjoy ourselves at Carnival when we see the State's Army constantly surrounding us in numbers. The same people who within the next year will forget our three days of cultural fun and harmony and turn back on us with their truncheons, handcuffs and vans. Seeing all this builds up tension and frustration within us.

The police, too, were fully aware of the rage and uneasiness their presence stirred among the young carnival goers and also of the severe criticism sometimes meted on them by the national press for their 'high handedness'. They did their best to present a friendly image. They sought to understand the ideology and traditions of the carnival. They sent police officers to attend the Trinidad Carnival, on which the Notting Hill Carnival was modelled, in order to learn more about its organisation and problems. In Notting Hill, police officers met regularly with the carnival organisers to seek their advice. In the 1984 carnival official orders were even given to members of the force to smile. Sometimes, a police band played for the carnival goers in the streets as well as at Westminster Cathedral where a Thanksgiving Service was performed on the eve of the carnival. Police men were invariably seen dancing with the carnivalists and were photographed being kissed by revelling black women. At one time they distributed badges with the inscription 'Mets are Magic' ('Mets' referring to the Metropolitan Police). Often, they also tried to abide by the request of the organisers to adopt a low profile and turned a blind eye to arrestable offences, particularly to the smoking of marijuana, which was publicly done by a large number of people.

They could not afford to under-police the area though. The organisers of the carnival who complained of police presence had, at the same time, refused to accept responsibility for maintaining order. In 1977 the hundreds of stewards they had employed had tried to control the youths, using sticks, but were instantly routed and beaten up; they had hurriedly taken off the uniform T-shirts which identified them as stewards and fled away. Subsequently, the stewards' function was only to help the mobile masquerading bands to proceed in orderly fashion along the prescribed route, and even in that limited task they were hardly effective.

So the police could not leave Notting Hill as a no-go area during the carnival. It was necessary to control crowd movements for safety, to protect the local residents and their homes, to guard the local shops and prevent violence from spilling out into the adjoining middle-class housing estates and commercial streets. There were also the tourists and other onlookers and revellers to safeguard. Also, although marijuana smoking was often ignored, it was not possible to tolerate the marketing of heavier drugs.

Thus, as time passed greater numbers of police, with ever more sophisticated strategies and techniques of policing, were mobilised for the event. The police force, of between 7,000 and 9,000, was divided into two parts. One part was kept as a reserve, temporarily housed in local schools and other public places around the area, ready with transport, and fully equipped with riot gear. The other part was dispersed among the crowd, every twenty men led by an inspector and two sergeants who communicated with each other and the police hierarchy in the control room with walkie-talkies.

The control room that was described by *The Independent* as resembling the operations centre for the Royal Air Force at the Battle of Britain,[6] was situated in a large gymnasium in a local school. Remote control cameras that 'could see in the dark' were installed to scan various sectors of the carnival area and relay pictures back to television monitors in the room. In front of the controller, a Chief Constable, each sector was represented on a board where the changing situation of the crowds and what was happening was shown. This continued to be the situation from 1977 to 1986. In the 1986 carnival a similar control room was set up, called 'Gold Control', 'gold' standing for central command, 'silver'

6. *The Independent*, 1 Sept. 1987.

and 'bronze' standing for divisions operating in the field under that command.[7] But Hurricane Charlie, brought in biting cold weather, torrential rain and strong wind that year, and played havoc with the carnival. Fewer people attended and the police command could not test the new system. Their broad strategy was to close all the streets leading to the Notting Hill area to traffic, except for the floats, and to close to both traffic and pedestrians some main streets that led to the centre of the Grove. Those streets were kept free for the reserve forces and the riot control units as well as ambulance cars to be rushed through from the periphery when trouble erupted.

The rest of the force spread among the crowds and were instructed to turn a blind eye to minor offences, such as handbag grabbing. (The police had forewarned the public not to carry valuables when attending the carnival.) It was difficult in a dense crowd to reach an offender and even if it had not been difficult it could be disastrous for the police to try to arrest offenders. Indeed, most riots in the past had started when the police attempted to arrest a black man. The young handbag snatchers did not operate individually but in organised gangs with elaborate strategies of action. Immediately after snatching, the snatcher was surrounded by other members of the gang and was rushed away to fade into the thick crowd. The gangs also had bricks and bottles which they hurled at any of the police trying to arrest their colleague. Some gangs of what the *Guardian* called 'Drapesers' wove among the crowds in single files like crocodiles of dancers;[8] they would surround a person and steal a purse or jewellery without making any attempt to hide what they were doing, relying on the force of their numbers, openly challenging the police. The police in the crowd or in the control room would see them but would be reluctant to take action. Sometimes they did react by sending trained 'snatching parties' who would attempt to grab one of the offenders, but that was very rare. The policy was not to react to individual offences. It was only when the gangs went beyond the limits that a large force was rushed into the spot to act with speed to prevent a full-fledged riot. As long as the incidents were sporadic and individual the offence was a 'criminal' act and ignored; when the incidents increased excessively and threatened to lead to larger scale rioting they became 'political' and the riot police were called in.

7. *The Telegraph*, 26 Aug. 1986; *The Times*, 23 Aug. 1986.
8. *The Times*, 1 Sept. 1987.

Towards the closing hours of Carnival Monday, 29 August 1987, the police decided that the rate of individual incidents had exceeded the tolerable level. The flashpoint came when, at about 8.30pm, officers tried to arrest a black youth in connection with an assault on a police sergeant. Bottles and bricks were thrown at them. Within minutes about a thousand policemen with riot gear rushed into action, in accordance with a well-rehearsed strategy. They were backed by armoured police vans and, because it was dark, a police helicopter beamed powerful searchlights on the crowds. A battle ensued. Many people were injured on both sides. During the two days of that carnival there were 798 reported crimes, one murder, 243 arrests for serious offences, 60 arrests for possession of offensive weapons, 13 police officers were taken to hospital for treatment and 76 civilians were injured, mainly as a result of gang attacks.[9]

There was an agitated political reaction from many national quarters with vociferous demands that the carnival should be banned altogether, or removed to a different area – a park or a stadium. An angry editorial in *The Times* laid much of the blame on the organisers for providing too few 'marshals', pointing out that 'one of the defining characteristics of a community is an ability to police its boundaries'.[10] It lamented 'the unfortunate fact' that leaders of the Afro-Caribbean population in London were ambivalent about the police and were thus exploited by these black men living a life of crime. It concluded that 'no civilized city can have need of such a great annual outburst of robbery and violence'.

The carnival became a major issue in the July 1988 Kensington parliamentary by-election in which the leading candidates called for tighter restrictions on the event. The Social Democrat candidate in particular predicted a catastrophe if it was not banned, unless the streets were cleared by dusk, unlicensed alcohol sales were ended and stricter rules on sound systems were introduced.[11] He was probably reflecting the interests of the 'yuppies' who had recently settled in newly gentrified houses in the area.

Thus the 1981–7 period was characterised first by the state attempting to co-opt the carnival; second by the structural integration of the stationary sound systems, as centres of intense cultural activities, with the mobile music and mas bands, among which the

9. *The Times*, 2 Sept. 1987, quoting Scotland Yard as source.
10. *The Times*, 1 Sept. 1987.
11. See *The Times* 11 Jul. 1988.

crowds – particularly with youths – moved all the time, going from one sound system to another, often temporarily acting as followers to a passing mas band. The carnival was thus an integrated unity of mobile and stationary sections. This was what made it different from Trinidad and Rio carnivals and what made the policing of the event a major problem. It was why, during the following four years, the police concentrated on completely separating the two sections, smashing the integrated unity.

5

The Carnival is Contained

The 1987–92 period saw the dramatic intensification of police activities against drug dealing and trafficking in Notting Hill, the containment of the carnival within a rigid framework and the dismantling of its structural unity, the challenge to West Indian claims to its sole 'ownership' and the mounting pressure for its commercialisation.

Events during the last three years of the decade indicate that the troubles of Carnival 1987 were not accidental but part of a new phase, brought about by a number of interrelated developments, with far-reaching consequences for the political, financial, cultural and ideological structure of the carnival.

To begin with, during the 1980s the particular political doctrines associated with the Thatcher governments (Thatcherism) brought about drastic changes in the British economy, with the intensive modernisation of its industry, the privatisation of nationalised industries, the encouragement of market competence, enterprise, competition and general self-help. Although the number of the unemployed soared, new types of jobs were created by the new technologies and the demand for suitably trained men and women to fill them steadily increased.

The new economic opportunities and the prosperity attending them benefited primarily the south-east of Britain, thus sharply intensifying the divide between north and south. The demand for housing in the south became intense and prices rose sharply. That eventually affected the Notting Hill area, which is situated in a central position in London, well served by all forms of public transport. Immense opportunities were opened for developers to buy old houses and convert them to luxurious flats to be sold at rocketing prices. Most of the new residents were 'yuppies' – Young Upwardly-mobile Professionals – ambitious and enterprising. They were particularly vociferous and articulate and soon formed a new force who joined with the developers and old disgruntled residents in agitating against the carnival.

At the same time, the police stepped up their campaign against the drug dealers who operated in the area, particularly in All Saints Road, where the Mangrove, which was still an important centre of carnival activities, was located. Early in 1987 a new, determined police commander, Chief Superintendent Clive Pearman, was appointed in the Notting Hill area. He soon launched a series of successful raids carried out by 4,000 members of his force against drug traffickers, followed by high profile policing. The Mangrove was raided in February and in May in what looked like a determined final showdown with Frank Crichlow and his supporters. About 150 police officers (some of them in riot gear and with dogs) sledgehammered their way into the building. The police claimed that they had found heroin as well as cannabis in Crichlow's pockets and also accused him of the more serious offence of being a drug-dealer and of using his premises for drug trafficking. He was arrested, his assets were frozen and he was kept in remand custody for six weeks until he was granted bail, pending trial, on condition that he be banned from attending his business at the Mangrove in the meantime.[1]

The trial was eventually held over a year later at Knightsbridge Crown Court and lasted for five weeks. Sixty-six police officers gave evidence under oath supporting the charges. But the defence argued consistently throughout the trial that Crichlow (as well as the others arrested in the Mangrove) had been framed by the police, that the drugs were simply planted on him, pointing out that his clothes had not been tested for traces of drugs, the drug packets were not finger-printed, his home never searched. The parish priest, a local doctor and a social worker gave evidence, testifying to his well-known efforts to combat drug dealing. There were testimonies about his cooperation with the police in the past, when he had often mediated between them and youths. The defence claimed that there had been a conspiracy, not just to destroy him but to destroy the whole West Indian community in the area in order to facilitate the rapid gentrification of that part of the inner city. The court procedure was halted several times, when the judge deemed that the defence had become too political. The

1. See *KN* 17 June 1989 and 22 June 1989.

trial ended on 16 June 1988. Crichlow and ten others with him were acquitted of the drug charges brought against them.[2]

Crichlow and other leaders of the West Indian community immediately went onto the offensive, charging the police with corruption, demanding the dismissal of the Notting Hill police station's commander, Pearman, the removal from the area of the sixty-six police officers who gave evidence at the trial and agitating for a public inquiry into police conduct towards the black community generally. Lee Jasper, of the National Black Caucus, was quoted by *The Independent* as saying: 'What has happened in Notting Hill is happening in black areas all over Britain. There seems to be a strategy of gentrification in the inner cities. Social engineering involving the police, local authority funding and agencies like the Task Force are being used to move the black community out of inner city areas'.[3] Crichlow himself said he would sue the police for damages, wrongful arrest and unlawful imprisonment.

These charges against the police came at a time when the British public had been shocked by scandals in which official investigators had found some police officers to have fabricated evidence in many cases in order to gain convictions. Juries in courts had become particularly suspicious of police evidence against black defendants. Probably nowhere else in Britain was that so starkly clear as in Notting Hill. In December 1989 a High Court jury awarded £100,000 damages to a West Indian, Rupert Taylor, a Notting Hill lay preacher, accepting the charge that the police had planted drugs on him when they had arrested him in 1984. He had been acquitted when the case had come for trial in Knightsbridge Crown Court in 1986. False imprisonment accounted for £10,000 of the award, £20,000 was for malicious prosecution and £70,000 to signify the jury's disapproval of the behaviour of the police. Another £100,000 was awarded against the police in court costs. Other similar cases were awaiting court action. An article in the *Kensington News* on those cases concluded: 'If public faith in the reliability of police evidence declines further, there is a serious risk that the guilty will go free as juries do not believe the evidence put before them'.[4]

In the meantime, the carnival had been facing the most serious direct challenge to its existence. On 1 August 1988, a few weeks

2. *KN*, 17 June 1989 and 22 June 1989.
3. *The Independent*, 23 June 1989.
4. *KN*, 14 Dec. 1989.

before the next carnival was due, a sustained and vigorous media campaign against the carnival and against the CAC was suddenly launched. It was triggered by the publication of a summary of a leaked report that had been prepared by management consultants Coopers & Lybrand, about the organisation of the carnival.[5] The report had been commissioned by the CAC but paid for by the Commission for Racial Equality. It contained a devastating criticism of the seven members of the governing body of the CAC, describing them as unprofessional, open to charges of corruption, 'laid back', representing neither the residents nor the performers and too feeble to exploit the tremendous financial potentialities of the festival. It recommended their replacement by fifteen trustees drawn from the performers, the local residents and the fund-providers.

The report unleashed a barrage of criticism in the national press, the radio and television, with the police spearheading the storm. Early in the year the police had reached agreement with the CAC, who had undertaken, among other things, to recruit 500 stewards to receive some kind of rudimentary training by the police. Now, in August, the police complained, only a few weeks before the carnival, there was no sign that recruitment had started. The police position was one of worry, not so much about actual crimes, but about public safety; they said they feared a stampede might be started by 'steaming gangs', causing a large number of people to be trampled to death.

The CAC retorted that they could not recruit stewards because the granting institutions – the Arts Council, the Commission for Racial Equality, the Local Councils of Chelsea and Kensington and of Westminster had not given them money. They claimed that those institutions had conspired with the police, not to release the funds unless the police were satisfied that their conditions had been met. They were vehement that 'the system' aimed at taking over the carnival. They also attempted to denigrate the report by pointing out an association between Coopers & Lybrand and South Africa.

In editorials, articles and news features the press dwelt on the extensive number of cases of mugging and robbing that had been carried out by steaming gangs during the 1987 Carnival, rejecting the usual black accusations of racism whenever they were criticised. Police officers pointed out that the split of the carnival into mobile

5. See *The Independent*, 1 Aug. 1988.

masquerading bands and stationary sound systems, with huge crowds milling chaotically between them, made policing an extremely difficult task. They denied that they were part of any conspiracy to ban or control the carnival, emphasising instead that what they were trying to do was to help establish a stable framework for a safe and trouble-free festival. That was to be achieved by limiting the number of sound systems, by siting them away from the route of the mobile bands, by directing these mobile bands to keep strictly to the official route and prohibiting their members from lingering within the area after completing their parade and by ensuring the recruitment and training of an adequate number of stewards. To achieve such a framework for the event would require a competent professional organisation.

Another theme in the campaign expanded on the criticism by the report of the consultants about 'missed economic opportunities'. The press harped on this issue and lamented that, instead of being a highly profitable business, the carnival was costing the British taxpayers hundreds of thousands of pounds each year.

Carnival 1988 was nevertheless held without a serious hitch and the CAC promised to study the report in due course and to follow some of its suggestions in preparing for the next carnival.

But in March 1989 the police raided the CAC office without any warning and took all records and accounts. They also searched the house of Victor Crichlow, who had acted as accountant for the Committee. An investigation into the finances of the CAC was started. The chairman, Alex Pascall, resigned and the CAC was put into voluntary liquidation, with debts totalling over a £100,000.

A new committee was immediately formed, the Notting Hill Carnival Enterprise Committee (CEC), which accepted the recommendations of the Coopers & Lybrand report and declared its aim of making the carnival 'work for the community'. The consultants' report had estimated that the carnival could yield large sums of income every year from fees from television companies, fees from licensing stalls, sponsorships by business companies and gala receipts. While gate fees could not be charged, it was estimated that about a quarter of a million pounds could be earned from the sale of a special 'carnival button' which could be sold at fifty pence each in pre-carnival parties and events as well as on Carnival Sunday and Monday. A five-year plan along these lines was drawn up, aiming both to make the carnival self-financing and a source of employment and income for the community.

The substitution of 'E' for Enterprise, in place of 'A' for Art in the new committee's title was not just a play with words. In its reincarnated form the committee represented a new clear ideology in the spirit of Thatcherism, emphasising competence, efficiency, competitiveness, rational organisation, initiative and profit.

The committee was now chaired by black barrister Claire Holder and prominent among its membership was Colin Francis, described in the media as Britain's top black civil servant, Director of the Task Force, a forceful yuppie – assertive, energetic, a true product of Thatcherism. They were part of a new breed of second generation West Indians who had adjusted to the institutional structure of the British system and succeeded in making the most out of the opportunities provided within it. From about the middle of the 1980s there had been a steady rise in the number of such successful individual black men and women. Diane Abbott, for instance, daughter of a metal worker and a nurse – who had immigrated into Britain in 1951, fought her way through A Level examinations, obtained a degree from Cambridge University and, after working as a civil servant at the Home Office, was elected to Parliament to represent the Labour Party in Hackney constituency and with the aspiration of returning to the Home Office, as Minister. Others had made it in business, advertising, acting, catering. A large number of black youths had been through various Youth Training Schemes (YTS).

The new committee was welcomed by the authorities. Grants to finance the forthcoming 1989 carnival were immediately pledged. An agreement was signed with the police, defining the route of the procession, the roads that would be closed during the celebrations, the number and positioning of the sound systems, details on street trading and the time the carnival should end. An indication of the degree to which the festival had been co-opted by 'the system' was that the new committee was patronised by the Conservative Member of Parliament for Kensington, Dudley Fishburn, who arranged for the 1989 carnival to be launched at a meeting in the House of Commons, in the full glare of media publicity and in the presence of potential sponsors of the event, with Claire Holder sitting as Chairperson. The meeting was marred by rebel activists who shouted abuse at the members of the new committee, calling them 'Black lackeys who were selling black culture to the establishment'.

A few days later, a 'Save Carnival' meeting was convened by the rebels at Tabernacle Community Centre, Powis Square, Notting

Hill, in which it was decided to stage a rival carnival in All Saints Road ('the Frontline'). Heading that movement was Frank Crichlow, leader of the Mangrove Community Association, who had just been acquitted of drug charges by the court.

The Carnival Enterprise Committee was denounced for taking 'black heritage and handing it on a plate to the establishment' as part of a conspiracy involving the police, the local council, property developers and the government's Task Force with the ultimate aim of driving the black community away from North Kensington. Its members were described as 'yuppie capitalists', 'coconuts', being dark on the outside but white inside, as 'black lackeys' selling black culture. Carnival was not about money, their opponents claimed, it was the expression of black identity and unity.[6]

Claire Holder was restrained in her reaction to everything that was said. The diatribe was continued in the main by a prominent member of the new committee, Colin Francis. He poured scorn on the 'conspiracy theory' and dubbed the Mangrove Community Association 'a group of ageing state-welfare dependent blacks', 'old guard' whose behaviour placed the black community in a ghetto. He urged the community to escape from 'the culture of dependency' and make the most of the opportunities that were open to them within the system.

The crisis on the eve of Carnival 1989 was temporarily averted when other community leaders persuaded the rebels to call off their plan to launch a rival carnival, with the promise of debating the issues involved when the impending carnival was over.

The carnival was duly held and, by all accounts, was the most peaceful ever; that is until it officially ended on Monday at 7.00 p.m. when, in conformity with the agreement with the police, the sound systems stopped playing. But hundreds of thousands of revellers lingered on, though many were on their way out of the area when suddenly trouble erupted in All Saints Road as a few young men attempted to gate-crash a party held in a private house. Some men from the house blocked their way to prevent them from entering and police approached the house to prevent violence. They were pelted with cans, stones and bottles. The police superintendent, who was in command in the area, notified his superiors that there was danger of a full-scale riot breaking out and asked permission to send in the riot police. Within minutes a large force,

6. See *KN* 27 Jul. 1989.

including over six hundred men in riot gear as well as a number of mounted police, stormed the crowds, most of whom were completely unaware of what was happening. Many found themselves trapped between police forces closing in on them from different directions.

It was obvious to most people that the police had over-reacted, to put it mildly. Despite that, there were renewed demands to ban the carnival, and under pressure from his conservative backbenchers, the Home Secretary called for a full report from Scotland Yard on the violence. Among the most persistent opponents of the event was John Wheeler, Conservative Member of Parliament for Westminster North, chairman of the all-party Home Affairs Select Committee, and of the Greater London Conservative MPs who had been calling for a ban for the past ten years.[7] He told reporters that the carnival was no longer a racial or local affair, but an international event which was advertised in the drug dealing streets of Amsterdam and which in general attracted people of a volatile nature. His views had been shared by many others including some white residents, the police and the local council.

However, as an editorial in *The Times* pointed out, the question of banning was a potentially explosive political issue which would cause more trouble than would allowing it to carry on.[8] It was not justifiable under the present circumstances and was probably not legally possible anyway. Another editorial in *The Times* a year earlier had shrewdly pointed out that one of the difficulties of banning the carnival was that it was badly organised, that if it had been competently organised in such a way that the organisers were in full control, it would have been possible to stop it. Such a view assumed that the organisers could have complete control over the crowds, though, that the carnival goers were somehow regimented, which was obviously not the case in such a massive popular movement. Indeed, it is in the very essence of Carnival that it is chaotic, that it is a celebration of disorder.

Instead of banning it, many pragmatists advocated reducing its size and restricting its movements, and that seemed to have been the aim behind the repetitively declared intention of the police to develop and institutionalise a stable, permanent framework for the event. That framework entailed the strict observance of an early hour for ending the celebration, the complete separation of the

7. See the *Guardian*, 17 Aug. 1988; *The Times*, 30 Aug. 1989.
8. *The Times*, 30 Aug. 1989.

mobile bands and the stationary sound systems and the reduction of the number of sound systems.

The new carnival framework dealt a devastating blow to the participation and operation of sound systems and ultimately to the attendance of tens of thousands of youths. The number of sound systems allowed to operate was cut by about 75 per cent, from about 160 sounds in the 1987 carnival to about 35 sounds in 1989. More significant was that the sound systems that were allowed to operate were those that had been affiliated within the British Association of Sound Systems. They were well-known sounds with a national professional reputation who were remote from local grass roots. On the other hand, most of those sounds that were not admitted were low-level, and came from different neighbourhoods of Greater London as well as from the provinces with their own local youth followers who in previous years had followed them to the carnival. To prevent 'pirate' sounds from operating in the carnival the manager of each of the officially admitted sounds had to display his licence. Stewards as well as police checked the identity and the positioning of the sounds.

The CEC accepted the police framework, which was duly adhered to during the following carnivals. It is indeed possible that on the part of the police, too, the decision to clear the crowds from the 1989 carnival was taken in order to stick to the agreed timetable. So strict were the rules that mas bands which arrived after 11.00 a.m. on Carnival Monday were prevented from entering the area because they were late. More seriously, followers who traditionally danced behind their mas bands were prevented from doing so. The Mangrove steel band was pinned down in All Saints Road for a long time on Carnival Monday because the truck driver was unable to manoeuvre the float through a narrow street in order to join the official mas band route. It was eventually allowed through when some other bands en route stopped and threatened to stay on the spot if the police continued to hold it. There were complaints from other bands.[9]

Thus, it was probably as a result of the strict rules contained in the framework that attendance in the 1989 carnival did not match that of previous years. The police estimate was that Carnival Sunday was attended by about 200,000 and Carnival Monday by about 600,000, though other sources quoted higher numbers of attendance. If the framework were to become the fixed structure of

9. For a compilation of such cases see La Rose (ed) 1989; 1990.

the carnival, attendance would certainly dwindle further, particularly as a result of the restrictions on sound systems.

More youths than those already excluded by the framework were excluded from the 1989 Carnival by direct police action against 'steaming gangs'. A special intelligence police unit had been gathering information on organised black gangs. During 1988 six such gangs of between twenty and fifty members each were said to have been identified and when police 'spotters' saw them on their video monitors approaching the carnival area they instructed police units on the spot to turn them back.[10] It is perhaps hard to imagine how accurate this remote control identification could have been and it is reasonable to suspect that an undisclosed number of groups of youths who were not members of such gangs were also turned back as it was almost always the case that youths from some neighbourhoods would come in groups.

Carnival makers complained of 'over organisation' and of the carnival being put in a straitjacket, in effect dampening the spirit of 'letting go' in an essentially chaotic genre of celebration.

Probably most serious of all was that the framework effectively dealt a death blow to the structural unity of the carnival by the rigid separation of the mobile bands and the stationary sound systems. The route for the mobile mas bands was delineated and the police insisted that they should stick to the official route, pass the judging points and leave without 'resting' in the area. The sound systems were sited away from that route.

The overall consequence for the entire carnival structure was dramatic. For, although in the past there had been an apparent cleavage between mobile bands and stationary sound systems, and despite the irritation caused by music jamming, the two sections had, over the years, integrated with one another within one politico-cultural structure. In this way the Notting Hill Carnival was fundamentally different in form from that of Trinidad. To begin with, over the years the sound systems had become centres of a live, developing, homogenised, all-West Indian culture. The many hundreds of stalls that flanked the sound systems exposed the revellers to the different foods and snacks of the various islands of origin, to black books, records, magazines, newspapers, photographs, clothing, paintings and religious objects. The revellers danced, talked and interacted. They were also addressed by the disc jockeys, the toasters, the poets about different themes that sharpened

10. See *The Independent*, 29 Aug. 1988; *The Times*, 29 Aug. 1988.

their consciousness of their oneness, particularly as together they faced their perennial enemy – the police.

Secondly, most of the mas bands were accompanied on the road by mobile sound systems, and because the pace of mobility was extremely slow, they became temporarily stationary and thus attracted more crowds. Most of the crowds moved in this way from one sound system to another, from mobile sounds to stationary sounds, or the other way round, doubtless feeling they were partakers in one and the same celebration. In effect, only the equipment of the sound systems and their operators and the stalls and their holders had been stationary. Nearly all the rest of the vast crowds were on the move, usually hopping from one stationary centre to another by latching on as followers behind a mas band on the way. Within the framework the mobility of the revellers was seriously restricted, particularly as the police also closed a number of streets that extended across the area.

There were bitter complaints against the restrictions and demands for investigations. On 6 September 1989 about a hundred people attended a meeting, called by Peoples War Carnival Band, at the Stroud Green Community Centre, Finsbury Park, to discuss police control of the 1989 carnival. Among those present were Frank Crichlow of the Mangrove Community Association, Victor Crichlow, treasurer of the now defunct CAC, Alex Pascall, former chairman of the CAC, John La Rose, director of New Beacon and chairman of Black Parents Movement, and representatives of several bands. The meeting was chaired by Michael La Rose, coordinator of Peoples War Carnival Band. Several band representatives described their experiences of police harassment in the course of Carnival Monday. Speakers argued that the police should not treat the carnival as a public order problem and should 'stay out of our culture', and that the performers should have a say in the conduct of the carnival.

A second meeting was organised by Ebony Mas and Pan, Cocoya Carnival Band, Eclipse Steelband, Mangrove Steel and Mas Band and Peoples War Carnival Band and was held on two weeks later at the Tabernacle Community Centre, Powis Square, Notting Hill. This was followed by a third meeting at the beginning of November, again at the Tabernacle Community Centre. After discussion it was unanimously decided to form an organisation to be called the 'Notting Hill International Carnival Committee'.

That committee held a meeting on 24 January 1990 to formulate a constitution. During the following months its members struggled for 'a People's Carnival'. They demanded the extension of closing time from 7.00 p.m. to 11.00 p.m., 'like the pubs', and greater freedom for people to move round the streets and dance behind floats.[11]

Claire Holder, whom the group described as 'a rubber stamp' for the police, told reporters that the group was a minority and was insignificant. At the same time she was also under pressure from certain of her own colleagues in the CEC to heed some of the criticism and the demands of the community. Her vice-chairman, Colin Francis, resigned in protest or exasperation, about a week before Carnival 1990, though he agreed to stay until the celebration was over. He complained of the 'total lack of management skill . . . lack of financial experience . . . and of the importance given to community street politics rather than to commercial decisions'.[12] He criticised continuous pandering to 'bogus community pressures', which he said would result in a continual cycle of no-growth and negative economic development.

During the months leading to the 1990 Silver Jubilee Carnival there was an attempt by the police to defuse the tension that had been created during the past three years. In January it was announced that Chief Superintendent Clive Pearman would be transferred to Scotland Yard.[13] His successor, Chief Superintendent Denis O'Connor, gave journalists the impression that he was critical of his predecessor's harsh approach. The *Kensington News* quoted him as saying: 'I think it's perfectly acceptable for Clive Pearman to have an opinion and to express it, but I think my own way is likely to be different'.[14]

The police also acknowledged that some mistakes had been made in policing the 1989 carnival, particularly in the rigid way the crowds were forced out of the area promptly at 7.00 p.m. They accepted the charge that they had not communicated their intentions to the crowds and promised the CEC to be more flexible and more communicative in the future. Also, in view of the bitter complaints against police surveillance helicopters which had hovered noisily over the area in past carnivals, a noiseless surveillance airship would be operated instead.

11. See the *Guardian*, 17 Aug. 1990; *The Times*, 25 Aug. 1990.
12. See *KN*, 23 Aug. 1990; *The Times*, 18 Aug. 1990.
13. See *KN*, 25 Jan. 1990.
14. 8 Mar., 1990.

In the 1990 carnival the police fulfilled their promises of a more flexible approach though their framework remained unchanged. During the following weeks relations between the black community and the police improved to such an extent that a black community leader, Jebb Johnson, Frank Crichlow's deputy, praised the police for their sensitivity and low profile stance.[15]

But the tranquillity did not last long. In January 1991 a terrible blow – what may prove to have been the deadliest ever – was dealt to the black community and to the carnival by the Royal Borough of Kensington, whose officers boarded up the Mangrove Community Centre's entrance and windows and securely closed the building because the centre owed the borough £71,643 in mortgage arrears. There was an outcry, with the Mangrove leadership accusing the borough of deliberately and premeditatedly conspiring with the police and the developers to silence the Mangrove once and for all. The council denied the accusation and declared that the building would be sold by public auction. The auction was held at the Kensington Hilton on 25 February. A consortium of local organisations headed by the Mangrove Trust bid against property developers from all over the country but was forced to stop bidding at £230,000. The building was finally sold for £277,000. An agitated Frank Crichlow told the *Kensington News*: 'There is a black cloud hanging over the community. . . . This was not a question of money, it was a question of politics. Both the police and the Royal Borough wanted the Mangrove out of the area'.[16]

The black community vowed that the spirit of the Mangrove would never die, and that they would soon acquire another building in the area, since they had raised enough money for the purpose, and indeed after a few months a smaller Mangrove surfaced.

Many carnival leaders thought that commercialisation of the festival was even more dangerous in its consequences than the police framework. The materialism that had been injected into the enterprise by the new leadership's acceptance of Coopers & Lybrand's recommendation to turn the carnival into a money-making business was insidious and threatened to transform the festival into a more formal, staged event, like the Lord Mayor's Show, nullifying its political significance. Money matters did have an effect

15. See *KN*, 1 Nov. 1990
16. For full details see *KN*, 31 Jan. 1991 and 28 Feb. 1991.

on the carnival in the past. Quarrels, suspicions and accusations about embezzlement of money by individuals had bedevilled the carnival every now and then, compounded by incompetence in budgeting and record keeping. The clamour for 'public accountability' had always been in the air.

The carnival had always relied on grants from public institutions. Also, for years, the organisers had attempted to persuade businesses to sponsor bands in return for advertising their products or services. Another element of financial consideration in the past had been the competition for prizes, as was the case with other carnivals in other countries. A substantial proportion of the budget of the CAC was earmarked for prizes. In every case organisers, bands and individual artists had to be careful not to antagonise granting institutions, sponsoring businesses or the panels of judges that awarded prizes. Never before, though, had money become the primary concern of the organisers.

The issue came to a head during 1991 when the major fund providers notified the CEC that in view of the current economic recession they had decided to phase out their grants within the following three years.

The crisis deepened the split in the carnival leadership, poignantly manifest on the eve of Carnival 1991 in dissension within the CEC. It was, in fact, a rift between brother and sister, Anton Holder, a member of the committee and Claire Holder the chairperson. (The *Kensington News*, 22 August 1991, sensationally referred to this as 'An unseemly family feud'.) Anton complained that the carnival had been divorced from the people and that not enough funds were reaching the performers. The Association for a People's Carnival charged that the carnival had been turned into a tame English-style parade and argued that the event should be guided and directed by the performers. Bluntly, but gently Claire Holder pointed out the economic realities of the situation and implied that without diligent economic planning to make the carnival self financing the celebration would not survive.[17]

Perhaps it was not an accident that the Report of Coopers & Lybrand had guardedly raised the issue of the 'ownership', and hence implicitly the control, of the carnival. It commented that the then current 'ownership' attitude towards the carnival by the then organisers (CAC) would have to be adjusted to the new realities.

17. See the *Notting Hill Carnival* magazine, 1991, p.3.

For the carnival makers that was potentially an ideologically as well as politically ominous threat, because it indirectly questioned the assumption made hitherto that the carnival was an exclusively West Indian monopoly.

The West Indians had tended to reify the concept of carnival, that is to treat it as if it were a material object, and to regard it as being exclusively their own, using the idea of 'ownership' in different senses depending on context of discourse. Thus Darcus Howe wrote: 'Carnival is part of the cultural and artistic expression of the slave community. . . . It is an outward expression of everything that is West Indian'.[18] Another issue of *Race Today*, which was edited by Howe at the time, was even more explicit, printing in large letters on the cover 'CARNIVAL BELONGS TO US' and using the same motto as the title of its editorial.[19] Musician Don Letts said: carnival 'is the one thing and one time that is ours and ours alone'.[20] Frank Crichlow, then director of the Mangrove Community Association, told journalists at a press conference that the newly formed Notting Hill Carnival Enterprise Committee (CEC) had 'taken black heritage [referring to carnival specifically] and handed it on a plate to the establishment'.[21]

The term was used in yet a different sense in the wake of the violent 1976 carnival, when the steelband men, the mas men and the sound system men left the old committee and formed the Carnival Development Committee (CDC) declaring: 'We are the Carnival. . . There can be no Carnival without us.' This was reiterated in 1991 by the Association for a People's Carnival when it declared that the carnival must be guided and directed by the performers.[22] Again, the theme of Carnival 1988 was 'Carnival is We Ting', meaning, as *The Observer* put it: 'Hands off. . . . it's ours'.[23]

The question of 'ownership' automatically led to the question of origin, of who had started the carnival. Until about the middle of the 1980s, Mrs Laslett had been acknowledged as the founder, the initiator, the first organiser of the carnival. The memory had still been alive in the minds of those who had lived in the area at the time, and Mrs Laslett herself was still alive and, although she was crippled with multiple sclerosis, continued to attend the cele-

18. Race Today.
19. Oct., 1976.
20. See the *Guardian*, 24 Aug. 1991.
21. *KN*, 29 June 1989.
22. *KN*, 22 Aug. 1991.
23. 21 Aug. 1988.

bration in a wheelchair. The masses of young carnival makers were in no doubt, though, that it was the West Indians who had started it. Latterly even first generation West Indians changed their view. They suddenly discovered that it had been a West Indian woman, Claudia Jones, who had somehow started the carnival.

Claudia Jones was born in 1915 in Port of Spain, Trinidad. In 1924 she was taken by her family to live in the USA, settling in Harlem, New York and living in poverty. She grew up to become a political activist, a leading communist. In 1955 she was arrested, tried, imprisoned, then deported to Britain, where she immediately became politically involved in the struggle against racism, almost single-handedly editing and managing *The West Indian Gazette* until she died in 1964, two years before the Notting Hill street Carnival started. Interest in her seemed to have been aroused by Buzz Johnson who had been researching for a short book about her: *I Think of My Mother*, published in London in 1985.[24]

The connection of her name with the carnival came suddenly in 1984 in the BBC's *Black Londoners* radio programme (which I happened to be monitoring at the time) in a remark by Alex Pascall, who was at the time chairman of the CAC. He promised to broadcast a sensational revelation about the origin of the Notting Hill Carnival within the following few days. A few weeks later Pascal mentioned her name in his Introductory Message to the 1984 edition of the annual journal, *Notting Hill Carnival*, as one of the founders of the carnival. It transpired that some time after the 1958 race riots Claudia Jones had arranged a big party for West Indians somewhere in London and that a competition between individual masqueraders was held at it. Victor Crichlow said he had attended that event and had won the first prize. He even displayed a photograph showing himself in his usual suit but with a hat in the shape of the Eiffel Tower on his head.

One seemingly reasonable answer to the question of ownership is that the carnival belongs to the carnival makers, i.e. to the people who attend the celebration. That might have been valid if all those who attended were active participants or performers. In the traditional sense of the concept all those who attended were supposed to play mas. In the Notting Hill Carnival, though, the overwhelming majority of those who attended did not play mas. Nearly all the whites attending the carnival were in this category. A more popular answer is that the carnival belongs to the community, and

24. See B. Johnson, *I Think of My Mother*, London, Kasia Press, 1985.

this seems to be the formulation given in the consultants' report. It is a vague statement, however, as it can mean different things: the Notting Hill black community, or the Notting Hill black and white community, or the black community in London or the black community in the whole of Britain.

As might be expected, the issue of ownership is highly sensitive because, hidden within it, is the fundamental political issue of who should control the celebration.

During the weeks leading to the 1992 carnival the subject was raised by 'the traditionalists' who claimed that the CEC had killed the carnival's unique spirit, that the celebration no longer belonged to the grassroots of the black community, that its control had passed to the police and the local Council. Jebb Johnson, a leader of the Mangrove Community Centre, called for the scrapping of the CEC and for its replacement by an old-style 'organisation for the people and by the people'.[25] But the CEC dismissed the opposition as a small minority and went ahead confidently planning the event, predicting a two million crowd and promising to outstrip the Rio carnival. The police declared that in view of the reduced crime rates in the 1991 carnival, they would reduce their forces by 5% in policing the forthcoming event.

The 1992 carnival was held (on 30 and 31 August) and despite bad weather attendance during the two days reached the million mark according to the organisers, although the police estimate was lower. There were fewer arrests than the year before. The carnival was indeed contained.

25. See KN 22.7.1992.

6

Communal Organisation

The division of the history of the Notting Hill Carnival into five distinct periods is to some extent arbitrary, because we are dealing here with a large-scale, ongoing politico-cultural movement within a continually changing complex post-industrial society. In this movement cultural forms and political issues are dynamically interrelated.

On the political side the years saw a steady mobilisation of West Indian men and women from different islands of origin, from different localities of residence within Britain and from different age groups. Attendance at the carnival on the Sunday and Monday of the August Bank Holiday sometimes reached the two million mark for the two days. Many of those attending as onlookers were white. Black attendance was regular and constant in size. White attendance on the other hand was irregular, affected by tension, the threat of violence, the attraction of other forms of entertainment and the vagaries of the Britsh weather. Since the 1970s the event had been organised and staged exclusively by blacks, under black leadership and the hundreds of pre-carnival events – parties, fetes, concerts, gala performances, calypso tents, mas camps, panorama competitions, house parties – were exclusively West Indian. For them the carnival had become a symbol of, as well as a mechanism for achieving corporate identity, unity and exclusiveness.

The West Indians had come to their 'Mother Country' to improve their life economically believing they would integrate within British society and culture without difficulty.[1] They did not need to develop an exclusive culture or to express a separate identity in terms of such a colossal corporate gathering as the carnival. However, growing unemployment and flagrant discrimination on

1. See E.Pilkington, *Beyond the Mother Country*, London, I.B. Tsawis, 1988.

the basis of colour in different fields and in almost every walk of life inevitably drove them to seek organisation and coordination for political action. The most efficient and effective way to do this would have been to develop a formal association in which the aims were clearly and precisely stated and the different organisational functions arranged rationally on bureaucratic lines. As many sociologists have shown, this is the most economical and efficient way of articulating the organisation of a corporate interest group, and the West Indians were fully aware of that as they demonstrated in the formation of hundreds of small functional organisations along these lines, such as the Black Parents Association, whose concern was for the schooling of West Indian children. But a variety of factors combined to inhibit the formal development of a corporate all-West Indian organisation of this type.

One factor was the division of the West Indians in Britain on the basis of their islands of origin. There *were*, certainly, many common factors affecting them. They were African in origin, their ancestors had been shipped across the Atlantic as slaves. They were exploited in plantation economies and suffered harsh repression under the colonial systems dominating them. The abolition of slavery in the mid 1830s had not changed their fortunes dramatically, nor had the independence of the islands after the Second World War brought salvation.

Nevertheless, the immigrants differed in a number of respects. The islands had been conditioned by different colonial cultures, English, French, Dutch and Spanish, and were also varied in the ethnic composition of their populations, in their size as well as in their geographical location and natural resources, and the major social, cultural and ideological divisions between the eastern and western islands.[2]

Immigrants to Britain had come from nearly all the islands, but the majority came from Trinidad and Jamaica. Although these two states had been influenced by British culture, they differed economically, demographically and politically. Thus, nearly half the population of Trinidad were East Indians, with those of African origin making up the other half. In Jamaica, on the other hand, the Africans were the overwhelming majority.

Trinidad's economic fortunes had been markedly improved after the Second World War by the discovery of rich oil deposits,

2. See S.W. Mintz, *Caribbean Transformations*, Chicago, Aldine, 1974 for a more detailed discussion.

80

while Jamaica had remained agrarian and poor. Also, after Independence, discussions about the formation of a Caribbean federation had given rise to rivalry for the dominance between these two islands, with Jamaica claiming leadership on the basis of population size and Trinidad on the basis of economic resources.

On the whole, there had been hardly any meaningful interaction between the islands, some over a thousand miles apart. The legacy of the plantation economy, which often relied on the cultivation of the single product (sugar), did not foster economic exchange between them.

When immigrants from the different islands had arrived in Britain, therefore, the main social interaction was between people originally from the same island. This natural island affiliation was solidified by the establishment of island associations that continued to play an important role in maintaining ties among the respective members, recreating parts of their particular cultures and maintaining strong links with people and groups back 'at home', as well as upholding a 'myth of return'. Island of origin orientation was further enhanced by the tendency for immigrants from the same island to seek residential propinquity in Britain. Thus many Jamaicans lived in Brixton, Trinidadians in Notting Hill, Dominicans in Paddington, though all always lived alongside whites.

Another factor that inhibited the development of a general West Indian political organisation was the nature of the British electoral system, conducted on the basis of local constituencies. Had elections been organised on the basis of proportional representation, the West Indians could easily have elected their own members of parliament whose voices would have effectively and systematically been raised about the particular issues affecting their community.

As it was, they were dispersed over many constituencies, in nearly all of which they were a minority within a white majority. It was, of course, possible for a major national party to nominate West Indian candidates as potential representatives of both whites and blacks within a constituency, and some West Indian activists have been clamouring for the establishment of 'Black Sections' within these parties in order to overcome the limitations of the electoral system. This has been particularly the case within the Labour Party, but so far the endeavour has met with strong opposition in one annual party conference after another, though the black members of the party continue to hold meetings and deliberations in separate forums which the party did not recognise. Overall this meant that the electoral system did not encourage the formation of an all-West Indian political organisation. Under the present electoral system, if West Indian candidates were elected, it would be their duty to represent the interests of both whites and blacks within the constituency. They would not be elected by whites who thought that their members of parliament would act parochially as a representative of West Indian voters only.

On their part, both major national political parties, Labour and Conservative, attempted to capture the votes of the black population, particularly in marginal constituencies where a small minority vote could be crucial in the success or failure of party candidates. The Labour Party concentrated its efforts in constituencies where large numbers of blacks lived among essentially working-class whites who were persuaded that a black representative in parliament would be as effective in representing them as a white candidate, and in the 1987 parliamentary election they succeeded in having two or three black candidates elected. The Conservative Party, on the other hand, could not rely on any substantial support from black voters in working-class areas. Instead they adopted a more subtle strategy by nominating for the 1992 election a black candidate, a barrister, in an almost exclusively white, affluent, middle-class constituency, thereby attempting to demonstrate to blacks nationally the possibilities of high achievements within the 'system', irrespective of colour. But the party faced a furious reaction from a substantial proportion of their white members protesting against the nomination and demanding reselection. One of the leaders of the protest was quoted as saying: 'I don't think we want a bloody nigger to represent us'. The members of the local party association decided to conduct a secret ballot over the issue to take place at 3.00 p.m. on Sunday, 10 February 1991. In the morning of that day readers opened their *Sunday Times* colour supplement to find the weekly feature 'A Life in the Day' devoted to the black candidate. There was a family photograph showing him with his white wife, a medical doctor, together with their three-year-old daughter. The text showed that the candidate had had an English education throughout, including his university degree, was highly informed, with an immaculately typical middle-class English life style. There was no trace of evidence to indicate that he interacted with blacks at all, although he had been serving as an adviser on race relations at the Home Office. Indeed the article seemed to be crying out loudly that 'He is one of us'. No wonder that at the ballot that afternoon two-thirds of the local party members who took part in the poll had heeded the call of the national party leaders and endorsed the nomination, and that many of those who voted against him affirmed later that, in the interest of party unity, they would rally in support of the candidate in the forthcoming election.

It is also possible to add to these factors inhibiting the development of an all-West Indian political organisation, the initial deep suspicion felt by West Indians for all formal organisations, a suspicion probably born out of past experience with white-led associations. They simply feared that any organisation they might join would enable 'the system' to control them. This was probably the reason why, for example, such a deep-rooted movement as Rastafarianism remained very largely unorganised. The Rastas simply carried God with them wherever they went and, apart from two numerically insignificant orgnisations – the Twelve Tribes of Israel and the Ethiopian Orthodox Church – the masses of Rastas in both Jamaica and Britain had not evolved an established church with a well-defined ritual hierarchy or a clearly recorded doctrine. The movement, massive as it was, was completely acephalous, decentralised, mercurial and elusive, leaving the police and the authorities in both countries completely in the dark. The movement's lack of effective corporate, coordinating mechanisms might have been its strength, though also its weakness.

But organisation need not be associative, based on a formal contract. It can be informally articulated through communal relationships and cultural forms supported by moral imperatives. The organisational functions of group, such as distinctiveness, authority and ideology, can be effected in terms of symbolic forms and performances that are based on primary, moral relationships. One of the most significant achievements of the studies of preindustrial, small-scale societies has been to show how, for example, stateless tribal societies (i.e. societies that had no central government), articulate a political structure in terms of the ideological symbols and ceremonial of kinship relationships and religion. Often in such societies, law and order are maintained by a balance of power between descent groups, with holy men mediating between them. Generally, associative relationships are segmental, involving only a part of the person, manipulative, utilitarian, non-moral, while communalist relationships on the other hand, are moral, non-utilitarian ones, in which men treat one another as ends in themselves. Few relationships are purely communal or associative; most combine the two, though in different proportions. Similarly, most organisations are both associative and communal, ranging on a continuum from the most associative, least communal, to the most communal, least associative.

A communalist organisation has no specifically stated aims, except in the most vague and ambiguous terms, and is not rationally and consciously arranged. As an *organisation*, it is clumsy, wasteful of the time and resources of its members and highly inefficient. For example, a formal medical association would discuss an issue by circulating an invitation to its members to attend a formal meeting, at a fixed date, time and place, with a fixed agenda. At the meeting, the issue would be discussed squarely, decisions taken, the meeting would come to an end and the members disperse to continue with their ordinary daily life. A communally organised political group, on the other hand, would meet to celebrate an occasion, such as the birth of a saint, the wedding of a member, or the commemoration of an ancestor, would engage in symbolic activities that had nothing to do with the issue, and would discuss the issue only informally and sporadically in the course of what, for the issue, were irrelevant activities.

In their struggle against racism, the West Indians tended towards the development of a corporate organisation through which that endeavour could be more effective. To achieve such a corporate organisation, they developed the potentialities of both associative and communal forms of organisation. The nearest they came to the associative form of corporate organisation was the formation of the West Indian Standing Conference, but this was a loose federation of over twenty organisations, and for a variety of reasons was feeble in its impact and had failed to gain the respect and loyalty of the masses of West Indians. No doubt in time a more effective associative organisation will evolve.

In the meantime they also embarked on varied and extensive efforts to develop a communal form of organisation. That was not a direct and conscious effort, but took the form of a search for common 'identity' and for an exclusive culture.

One form of communal organisation found extensively in small-scale preindustrial societies is that based on a predominantly kinship-and-marriage ideology, which under some circumstances can also be adapted to modern conditions, though not necessarily as a major articulating principle. Indeed, kinship and marriage are intimately involved in the political process in all socities and contribute, to a greater or lesser extent, to all communally-based organisations. This can be seen clearly even in a large-scale post-industrial society like Britain. For example, legislation facilitating or discouraging divorce, child allowances, the taxation of wives separately from husbands, the obligation of a begetter to contribute to the maintenance of his children, state pension, and so on, affect the kinship structure and the distribution of income and of power. This is not a one-way process, because men and women resist some of these laws in a variety of ways, either at the formal national level by, for instance, supporting a political party which can agitate to change the law, or at the individual level as, for example, in the resistance of some men to paying maintainance for the children they have fathered. The government may choose to react to this by proposing legislation that would enable the courts to arrange to deduct child support from the father's income. This might eventually cause men who father children to deny paternity. And so on.

The West Indians observed no lineal descent principle, but their patterns of conjugal relationships had the potentialities for creating an extensive web of cross-cutting ties which could contribute to their communal arrangements.

There is a great deal of controversy about the 'traditional' structure of kinship and marriage among working-class Afro-Caribbeans.[3] The pattern reported for many of the islands is that of great instability of conjugal relations. According to this pattern, a woman would start her mating career at an early age, often bearing children by different men, before settling down in a formal marriage. A man would similarly father a number of children by different women before marriage, at a late age, and would continue to have out-of-marriage liaisons that might produce more children even after marriage. This pattern of unstable conjugal relationships had been dictated by uncertainty and instability of employment among males. It had nothing to do with 'race'. Scholars demonstrated that white communities living under similar economic conditions developed the same pattern of unstable conjugal relations.[4]

When the West Indians came to Britain it was assumed, largely

3. See MacDonald and MacDonald 'The Black Family in the Americas: A Review of the Literature', Sage Race Relation Abstracts, no.3, 1978, pp.1–42.
4. For a survey see MacDonald and MacDonald, 'The Black Family'.

a priori, that, after exposure to British society, and with the change in their economic fortunes, they would develop more stable patterns of family relationships; and some early researchers affirmed that there was empirical evidence that more West Indians were marrying when young and that their marriages were more stable than in the past. However, as the years went by new factors developed and inhibited those trends.

To begin with, most of the West Indians who came to Britain were from the working classes; as the middle classes from their islands had gone to North America, and it has only been recently that a small, new middle class has been emerging among them and some of these are indeed marrying young. Secondly, a great deal of conjugal instability developed in the meantime among the white British population, with about a third of marriages ending in divorce. The same population saw a dramatically rising number of families with dependent children headed by a single woman and an increasing proportion of young couples cohabiting and even having children without formal marriage. The contribution of the West Indians to the overall statistics in this area is minimal, because they are only a small proportion of the total population. Thirdly, the availability of social security benefits in support of unmarried mothers for both income and accommodation has greatly encouraged working-class girls, both white and black, to seek independence from parents by becoming unmarried mothers at an early age. Fourthly, unemployment, which grew during the 1970s and 1980s, seriously discouraged men from settling down in marriage. For their part, many women were not prepared to marry men who did not have stable employment. West Indian men in particular suffered from higher rates of unemployment. Relatively more West Indian women were employed than men and that, together with their guarantee of stable accommodation, strengthened their independence and their power *vis-à-vis* the men. This was a departure from the 'traditional' pattern back in the West Indies.

The pattern that emerges from all of this is one of relatively stable women-headed households, with men erratically moving from one woman to another. These statements about conjugal relations in the Caribbean and in Britain are largely based on general impressions and fragmentary empirical research. A variety of methodological and practical difficulties have made comprehensive empirical research problematic. In Britain, the regular population census, taken once every ten years would have shed a great deal of light on developments in kinship and marriage among the West Indians were it not for the fact that, since the 1970s, any mention of race or of ethnicity in the census has been prohibited by law, though birthplace is mentioned. This was rectified in the 1991 census, the results of which had not been made public at the time of writing.

Thus it was not possible to undertake a systematic empirical study of kinship and marriage for the present study. Instead, detailed biographies and social networks of a small number of men and women were collected. For that purpose a comprehensive form was constructed, covering age, birth place, sex, father's birthplace and mother's birthplace, number of years in the United Kingdom for both Ego, mother and father, education and training, occupation and other sources of income, history of conjugal relations, children by age and sex, accommodation and household arrangements, active kinship relationships, active friendship relationships, leisure activities and interests and religious affiliation and activities.

The interviews were open-ended, with the form only indicating the relevant information needed. The data were collected within one neighbourhood in West London by a research assistant who had lived and worked as a community official in the same area for ten years and had personally known the interviewees, so that part of the data were from her own observations and knowledge. In all, twenty men and women were covered.

It is obvious that these men and women did not constitute a sample of the West Indian community. Each of them was a distinct personality in his or her own right. What was sociologically significant was to look for the nature of the interconnections between the salient features of their biographies, such as employment, conjugal relations, and present social networks.

One of the most important consequences of *these practices* in kinship and marriage is the multiplicity of cross-cutting links that they generated and the flexibility of household membership. A man can trace relations with full siblings, sets of half siblings, numerous cousins, 'uncles' and 'aunts', grandmothers and, to a lesser extent, grandfathers. These relations cut across and overlapped, creating a dense network of potential relationships. The strongest of these relations were those between mother and child and between full siblings, though in some cases the other relationships were equally strong.

There was no clear system of norms, values, obligations and

duties consistently associated with weaker relationships, although there was a notion that all relatives ought to help one another. It should be remembered that we are dealing here mostly with unemployed, partly-employed or lowly-paid employed men and women who have no spare financial resources to pass on through the kinship network when the need arose. The availability of regular state benefits, meagre though these could be, limited the material significance of these links. The overall result was that there was no well-defined body of values, beliefs, norms and symbols that would have expressed, objectified and kept alive the total network as a system. However, the network was morally and politically significant in that it served as a potential system of communication as well as an additional basis for community sentiment and obligation.

A much greater organisational potential for such groups is often provided by religion, which has served the development of communal organisations among different groups in both industrial and pre-industrial societies, past and present. Religion and religious organisation and leadership played a crucial role in the development and organisation of the Civil Rights Movement among the Blacks in the United States during the 1960s. That lesson was not lost on the West Indians in Britain.

When they came to Britain they had been initially confident that they would be welcomed by the established churches as part of their regular congregations. But when they flocked to a church, white worshippers moved away to other churches. That eventually led to the development of all-black churches, which often encouraged the revival of traditional West Indian forms of worship. A nationwide association of Black churches was eventually formed. A lay preacher even talked of the necessity of developing a Third Testament to record the tribulations of black people in the course of four centuries of enslavement, oppression and savage discrimination.

The potential for formal religious institutions to articulate communal organisation are immense, but were limited among the West Indians in Britain. First, being Christian in a predominently Christian society, their distinctiveness as an exclusively religious community was not sharp. Secondly, internal denominational differences inhibited full unity. Thirdly, not all West Indians were religious or churchgoers. Attendance at services was predominently by women and children; most men did not attend and working-class youths in particular were absent. Even those of them who were devout Rastafarians did not participate in regular congregations. Class differences were also manifest in religious practice. Middle-class families attended ordinary quiet service, sometimes in mixed churches together with whites, but there were few of them. Those families were integrationist; they had either 'made it' or were on the way. They owned houses, had bank accounts, had mortgages, pushed their children to achieve in higher education. In short, they had become part of the native system and were trying to make the best of the opportunities it offered. They were not particularly pre-occupied with racism.

In the mid-1980s gospel singing caught the imagination of the new middle-class youth and was glamorised both by a concert held at the Royal Albert Hall and by a highly impressive BBC television prime time viewing Sunday programme in the 'Songs of Praise' series, conducted by Ian Hall. However, the movement only involved a small minority and did not seem to attract the masses of working-class youth.

Rastafarianism was of more political significance as a West Indian religious movement. It spread widely among youth during the 1970s and the first half of the 1980s. It did radicalise the youth and mobilise them for opposition to 'Babylon', viz., the British establishment. Babylon was conceived as a decadent and corrupt system which lay beyond the boundaries of morality and against which any act would be justifiable.

For a variety of reasons, though, the movement was incapable of serving as an articulating principle for an all West Indian corporate organisation. In the first place, it alienated its followers from British society by its call for the return to Africa. That meant that they were not concerned with organisation for operation within, and in terms of, the British political system. (That would contrast sharply with the theme of a masquerade of Peoples War Carnival Band in a carnival in the mid 1980s: 'Come what may; we are here to stay'.)

Secondly and more seriously, the movement was not clearly defined or delineated. It had no unified doctrine, nor a ritual hierarchy. It had no coordinating organisation. The large number of youths who donned the colours of the movement, grew their locks, smoked marijuana and danced to the sounds of reggae, thus signalling identification with the movement, differed subjectively in their faith: many entertained no mystical beliefs relating to the movement at all and were repeatedly disowned by those who claimed to be the genuine believers. Its identification with West Indian youths relates to its third reason for failing to provide a voice for West Indians as a whole for it was generally a movement of youth and did not embrace many adult men and women.

Fourthly it relegated women to an inferior position at a time when they had become the pillars of the West Indian community and were financially better off than the men. More males were dependent on females than the other way around.

Thus neither kinship nor religion could articulate an all-West-Indian organisation. On the other hand, the carnival, 'frivolous' as it seemed, had proved in that respect to be more powerful and efficacious, both culturally and politically. It subsumed and politicised many cultural and aesthetic forms. A great many traditional forms were revived, not as regression to the past, but to serve new purposes. The Trinidad carnival conventions had been developed in the course of a century-and-a-half of experience and of trial and error.

Carnival taps, shapes and manipulates deep and powerful emotions, passions and sentiments. Revellers frequently stated that during the carnival they 'let go . . . relax . . . forget about the problems of ordinary daily life . . . escape from pressure'. They say: 'It is the only occasion I forget about Giro and the DHSS . . . I feel that I am light and up in the clouds. . . It is the joy of complete abandon'.

The beating of the drums, loud music, jumping in dance, smoking marijuana and drinking alcohol, as well as being part of a large crowd, conduce to ecstacy and deepen this feeling of liberation from social constraints generally. One of the leading mas designers at the Notting Hill carnival, Larry Forde, told me once that Westerners did not know how to relax and that one of his artistic ambitions was to design and choreograph a masquerade demonstrating this theme by enacting the Biblical story of the Golden Calf, when in the abscence of Moses on Mount Sinai, the Israelites burst out of dogma and discipline and created a corporeal god in the form of a golden calf and indulged in an orgy of dance, revellery and desires around it. Carnival occasions a variety of playful activities which some writers believe to be an aspect of human nature and Turner,[5] citing Huizinga's *Homo Ludens*[6] seems to explain carnival in these terms.

Women in particular, after a year of domestic and social pres-

5. V.W. Turner, 'Carnival in Rio' in F.E. Manning (ed.) *The Celebration of Society*, 1983.
6. J. Huizinga, *Homo Ludens*, Boston, Beacon Press.

sures, are allowed to 'let go' into an ecstatic mood, exhibiting bawdy behaviour and dancing in a sexually provocative manner. There is also indulgence in eating and drinking.

These manifestations of revelry are not instinctive, in the sense of being spontaneous and expressive of inherent natural character- istics, but are culturally defined and structured. They cannot be accounted for in terms of the psychology of the individual. It is not the case that all the hundreds of thousands of people, separately and intersubjectively, suddenly and simultaneously reach the limits of psychological tension in their everyday life, so that they all auto- matically and spontaneously burst into a frenzy of playfulness and unrestrained lust. The dates, times, conventions and forms of play are fixed externally by the collectivity. On the eve of the carnival people would have been through different circumstances, with dif- ferent moods. But no matter what their inner moods and feelings had been, they would generate, on the specific dates and at specific times, the 'right' cultural forms and the right feelings for engaging in revelry and jollification. Indeed, it is often ritual that conjures up subjective beliefs and meanings, not the other way round. This is not to deny the reality of the 'psychic factor'; or to assume human nature to be a *tabula rasa* on which culture inscribes its dictates. The psychic energy is certainly there in the individual, but it is given definition, shape and direction by the culture, which is itself informed and manipulated by political and economic interests, imperceptibly playing a crucial part in this whole process, adding further 'motives' and 'drives' to the impelling psychological 'life force'.

This point has been accentuated here to clarify the controversy surrounding the so-called safety-valve theory which treats carnival as a cathartic mechanism provided by the system or the ruling class to expunge peoples' bitterness and emnity against the prevailing social order.

7

The Political Dimension of Art and Music

The Notting Hill Carnival capitalised on the fundamental role that music had played in the history and daily lives of the West Indians. During slavery their masters had deprived them of their traditional culture, destroyed their religion, prevented them from communicating with each other. But they were allowed to sing and play music, most probably because music and singing were deemed conducive to sustained hard work. The slaves thus preserved and developed many of the musical forms that had permeated social life in their countries of origin in West Africa. Eventually they developed the traditional pattern of the 'praise and scandalising singer' to pour scorn on their masters and to conspire against them. Music was their means of communication, resistance, entertainment and secret ritual. Drumming, in particular, was highly developed, which was the reason why the masters did not approve of it and sometimes banned it. In West Africa drumming had been a 'language' in its own right, an effective means of communication. The Yoruba of Nigeria, for example, had developed 'the talking drum' into a highly sophisticated instrument. The skin of the drum was held to the curved body of the instrument by strings. The drummer held the drum under his shoulder with his arm around it so that by pressing his arm on the strings he would vary the tension of the skin and thereby produce variations in pitch, mimicking speech.

It was perhaps no accident that the West Indians eventually invented the pan, the basic instrument of the steel band, and transformed it into such a powerful cultural and political symbol, and that it was the Notting Hill Carnival that initiated, developed and sustained the steel band movement in Britain.

The development of the steelband movement in London was in many respects a sociological puzzle. First, because of the incongruity of such a crude, clumsy and noisy instrument existing at all in one of the world's most advanced and sophisticated music centres, under essentially intelligent middle-class West Indian leaders. Secondly, because its development was so rapid in the 1970s, although the music had been familiar for long before that.

From about 1973, steelband music became a massive movement, and in the course of a few years, something like one hundred bands came into being, involving hundreds of players and thousands of supporters and followers, most of whom had nothing to do with it in Trinidad. The initial impetus came from Leslie Palmer, who urged the formation of steel bands for participation in the Notting Hill Carnival.

More striking was the resistance of the majority of West Indian steelband men to any rationalisation or standardisation in the production of the pans, in tuning them, and in the basic organisation and musical coordination of the band. The making of pans was so haphazard that it is no exaggeration to say that no two pans were alike. Each pan was an individual instrument: the metal of the oil drums might be different, and hammering the base to sink it was done crudely and had different results each time. Sometimes the base was torn in the process and the whole drum was cast away. But making the pan was still a simple task, compared to tuning it. Tuning was the most expensive and problematic stage in preparing the instrument. Tuning a piano in the mid-1980s in London cost about £20.00, but tuning one single pan cost about £80.00, though it could cost a little less if all the pans of a band were tuned together. Moreover, while the piano remained tuned for months, the tuning of a pan was so delicate that if it was dropped to the ground, or roughly knocked about, it would be spoilt and would have to be retuned. There were calls for mechanisation and standardisation in making and tuning the pans, but many of the musicians maintained that the product would not be the same; that it would be a different instrument altogether.

There was also resistance to the writing of the music. Usually the music was composed by a calypsonian and learned by a band with initial help from the arranger. Steelband men could not be taught by formal instruction, but only by practical demonstration. Generally the band learned to play a piece by trial and error. The players had no conductor but adjusted their playing to one another. You listened to your neighbour and looked at him playing, argued with him if necessary and then coordinated your sounds with his. If he was not performing well you went to him, took his stick and demonstrated, and so the rehearsals went on for months until the piece was learnt.

The threat of rationalisation and standardisation came principally from the racially mixed state schools of the inner cities which adopted steelband music as part of the curriculum. There had been a great deal of pressure on the schools to develop multiracial or multicultural education. The academic underachievement of West Indian children at school had alarmed parents, teachers and the educational authorities. West Indian leaders argued that one of the reasons for their failure was the imposition on West Indian children of an English education with its traditional value system, which implicitly denied the significance and validity of their own West Indian culture. There was, therefore, a demand for the recognition of West Indian cultural identity and the encouragement in the children of pride in their heritage, to give them confidence and encourage them to achieve greater success in their learning. Many schools tried to cater for that demand and duly introduced West Indian topics in their history, literature, art and music courses, and among those had been steelband music, which many schools in the inner cities began to perform in their own newly-formed bands.

The first teachers were recruited from among the professional West Indian steelband men. The Inner London Educational Authority even appointed a well-known senior steelband leader, Forsyth, as adviser to supervise the school bands and hold meetings with the newly appointed teachers.

What no one bargained for, though, was the fascination that the steelband music presented to many white children and teachers. At first this gave pride to the West Indians. In many of the schools the steel bands were racially mixed, but some had predominantly white players and in a few there were white players only. A number of white teachers enthusiastically learned and began to teach steelband music and a number of music teachers, both black and white, began to rationalise it, to write the music down and play it under a formal conductor. By doing so, however, they changed the whole character of the band and of its music. That drove many of the black students away from the racially mixed bands, particularly when those bands were led by white teachers. The black teachers became, to some extent, divided: a minority supported the rationalisation while a majority resisted it. Resistance also came from the professional bands outside the schools.

Their opposition was not prompted by conservatism or ignorance. On the contrary, it was voiced by enlightened and fully conscious leaders. What was more, the professional 'traditional' bands outside the schools had not been sitting idle on their pans and music, but had been continuously inventing and developing new forms. Indeed, it was the rationalisation that was likely to ossify and eventually destroy the steelband movement, and thereby, in effect, neutralise the political movement which it helped to articulate.

This is because the issue that was involved was political, not just musical. The steelband movement was both political and cultural, with both processes dynamically intertwined, with a change in either process likely to affect the other. Thus, rationalisation in the production of the pan, in the composition of the music and in the organisation of the band, would inevitably have led to the subordination of steelband music to Western musical conventions, and that would have led to the containment and the integration of the men and women involved in it within the hegemony of the established order.

To follow this line of thinking, we must shift our attention for a while from the music to its social dimension. Looked at in this way, the music can be seen as an instrument for the development and maintenance of a social collectivity, with its network of interpersonal relations of amity. The music helped in the mobilisation of the collectivity and the collectivity developed the music further.

To begin with, the elementary form of the pan and of the band necessitated intensive face-to-face interaction among the players. Each member had to coordinate his playing with that of the other members, as there was no conductor and no written scores. In the process, a strong bond of loyalty developed among the players. Each band also had a number of reserve players, to make up for the absences or act as additional players on the occasions when a larger set of pans was used. The band also had a large number of admirers, followers and supporters who frequented its performances and revelled behind it in street processions. In the months of preparation for the carnival, the band was linked with a mas band, playing in its precarnival parties and accompanying it on the road on carnival days.

There was a great deal of informality in the performances. In the carnival procession the band played continuously for many hours, with individual players stopping every now and then to have a drink, a smoke or a sandwich or to chat with someone, and then resume playing. Players and dancing followers became ecstatic and swayed in a vigorous communion with it.

An established band was also usually linked to the workshop of a pan maker and tuner. Sometimes the band started by making its own pans. In some other cases the pans were owned by a pan maker who was one of the founders of the band, but in the majority of cases the professional bands owned their own pans corporately, so that the pans ensured continuity despite the frequent change of personnel. The overall effect was that there was no alienation between the instrument and the player, who was always at least aware of the processes by which the pan was produced.

Another feature of steelband music was its association with calypso.[1] Calypso songs usually contained social commentary and followed the traditional West African institution of the Praise Singer, who sang the praises of his patron and castigated the weaknesses of his opponents. The calypsonian was a poet and musician at one and the same time, and the two roles affected one another in the development of the steelband music. Many of the popular steelband tunes were composed by calypsonians. The music was moulded to articulate the words of the poem, which was always in patois, an English-Caribbean dialect. Even when the calypsonian was absent from the scene the steelband music seemed redolent of his words. This association of the steelband music with words of social comment in the vernacular should explain why many steelband men shrugged their shoulders when they listened to a steel band playing European tunes, saying: 'This is not steelband music'.

The steelband movement developed into a symbol of protest against white society in the inner city. The making of the pan involved a great deal of sustained noise and the strong smell of burning tyres and there was also noise involved in the rehearsals. The impact on whites in the neighbourhood of steel bands had been devastating and had always given rise to complaints and opposition.

What was sociologically significant, however, was that although steelband music had been developed in Trinidad, and was introduced into London by Trinidadians, in Britain it had now involved Trinidadian-born men who had had nothing to do with it back at

1. See Warner 1982.

home, immigrants from other islands and British-born West Indians generally. Some of the steelband men in London did have links with other steelband men in Trinidad and elsewhere, but soon developed a high degree of autonomy of their own. The tuners established and organised a British monopoly by deciding to boycott the handling of any pan which had been manufactured in Trinidad, or elsewhere, preventing pans made by cheap labour in the West Indies from being imported to Britain.

It is clear from the foregoing account why there was resistance to rationalisation and standardisation in the manufacture of the pans. Modernisation would have alienated the instrument from the player, standardised the pan and thereby sealed the continuous creative experimentation made possible by the individuation of the instrument. More significantly, the introduction of music scores and band conductors would have changed the structure of the band; instead of communal relationships developing among its members mainly diadic relationships would have developed between conductor and player. Writing down the score would have subsumed the music under the hegemonic tradition of European music and would, in time, have relegated it to a narrow, inferior status. The link between the music and Caribbean dialect, and hence the lyrics of the calypsonian, would have been severed. The music would have been quieter and gentler, and its symbolic effect would have changed. The ecstacy that the music created in its players, followers and audiences would have weakened. Perhaps more significantly, its leaders would have lost their independence and come indirectly under the control of state educational institutions. In short, by becoming rationally organised, the music would have ceased to be a people's music and its political impact would have been lost. Indeed it was adopted by the West Indians in London in the first place *because* it was non-rational. Steelband music would have ceased to be such a powerful political movement if it had accepted such changes. In Trinidad, steelband music was brought indirectly under the control of the state. On the advice of the government, the bands were financially sponsored by the local branches of multinational corporations and their members were given a fixed number of jobs in each case. The CDC, the Carnival Development Committee, was a government agency which controlled the preparation and staging of the carnival. The competition between the bands for substantial prizes every year, in an event called PANORAMA, transformed the steelband music from an essentially street music to a stage music. The *Trinidad Carnival* magazine lamented those developments, saying that the carnival and its music were no longer a people's movement.

In a book entitled *Art, an enemy of the people*, Roger Taylor argues that when popular cultural movements are made to imitate high culture they are thereby destroyed as peoples' culture.[2] Art is far from being a universal essential practice; it is a solidly upper class practice. Taylor castigates not only bourgeois societies but also Marx, Lenin and the communist state for upholding high bourgeois art as a value to be inculcated in all people in a socialist society. As a demonstration of his arguments, he traces the history of jazz in America, showing how in the process 'even the American establishment takes jazz up, supporting it as America's unique contribution to the arts'.[3] He concludes that this capture of jazz by the art tradition brought about the decline in jazz as popular experience, for jazz was changed by the new outlook of its players.

This is undoubtedly an exaggerated stance, but it highlights the nature of the contradictions that are implicit in the steelband movement in Britain. Among the West Indians there were those who proposed rationalisation and integration. A prominant leader of the integrationists was a West Indian music teacher, who organised a band out of school which he called 'orchestra'. His uniformed band was modern, playing both classical and popular music. He was always dressed in a suit and tie and carried a briefcase, had a formal visiting card, was very industrious and pressed the educational authorities to treat steelband music as an official musical form, not only in teaching but also for the purposes of public school examinations. He founded an association of steel bands, complete with a governing body consisting of a group of dignitaries and a periodical newsletter. His band was frequently invited to play in formal gatherings, including at services in Westminster Cathedral, and appeared on BBC television. His association was boycotted by the professional popular bands, though, and most of the black-led school bands, whose leaders described him as a 'culture-vulture', an opportunist who was only jumping on the band wagon.

The carnival also mobilised, manipulated and integrated the originally Jamaican sound system, its music and its culture, bring-

2. R. Taylor, *Art, An Enemy of the People*, Hassocks, Harvester Press, 1978.
3. *Ibid.*, p.153.

ing to Notting Hill a whole new generation of rebellious West Indian youths and thereby changing its own structure from the traditional Trinidadian form. A session combined dancing, drinking, marijuana smoking, the dissemination of important news and the pronouncements of Rastafarian views and sentiments.

The sound system was certainly the most important West Indian institution in the inner cities. It consisted of a record player, an amplifier, a number of speakers and a collection of records. The larger and more powerful these were, the more important the sound system – or 'sound'. Involved with the sound were its manager, disc jockey (DJ), toaster, operator, helpers, followers and general audiences. There was a marked emphasis on the bass, which was so powerful that it not only penetrated people's bones, but literally shook the building in which it operated.

Sound systems differed in size and power and in the sophistication of their electronic equipment. They also differed in their record collections. The use of multitrack techniques by recording studios enabled them to isolate the various instrumental and vocal sounds in recorded music. That made it possible to vary the musical structure of a piece in numerous ways, by omitting certain sounds in the original recording or by changing the volume of different tracks. The result was that there were different versions of the same piece and this enabled the DJs to cater for different audiences. Some of those versions served as background for the toaster who might be reciting poetry or just talking in comment on current events or philosophising about life and about society. The DJ also had sound effects under his control, such as thunder, police car sirens, etc. Such technical flexibility made it possible to adjust the sounds to the taste and moods of different audiences.[4] The sound systems also differed in scale, from small local systems operated by a few amateurs to powerful systems professionally operated and catering for a large sector of the metropolis. There were elaborate and noisy competitions between sound systems on the bases of sound volume, record collections and the skill and artistry of the operators. Every system developed a core of loyal followers.

Thus, when the sounds were called on in the middle of the 1970s to participate in the carnival they brought with them the tens of thousands of youths who had been their followers. For months before the carnival the sounds kept their audiences

4. See D. Hebdige, *Cut 'N' Mix*, London, Comedia Books.

informed about the forthcoming carnival in precarnival parties, fetes and seminars. There was no precarnival party that did not have one or more systems playing, often together with a steel band. In time, they played calypso and soca records along with the usual reggae pieces. When the systems became mobile, some of them organised their own mas section. They also became involved in the politics of the carnival, in relations with the police and in the struggle for funds. Their leaders became involved in internal politics, in the rivalries and competitions in the organising committees. During the 1980s' carnivals they even tended to overwhelm the steelband-accompanied masquerading bands by the volume of their sounds until they were forced to form their own assocition and have representatives from it on the organising committee who would restrain association members from spoiling the carnival for the mas bands.

Although originally associated with Jamaica and Jamaican music, the sound systems became generally British-Caribbean. The La Rose brothers of People's War Sound System were Trinidadian, yet they were among the pioneers in running a sound system which in its earlier years played mainly reggae music. Even more interesting was the development of mainly soca-playing sound systems, many of which became mobile for the carnival. Lord Sam was one of the first to invest large sums of money to render his soca sound system mobile. Many others followed him in doing the same. Those soca-playing mobile sounds were more suitable for carnival than the usual, mainly reggae-playing sounds. An indication of the rapid growth of soca-playing sound systems was the formation in 1984 of the Association of Soca Sounds.

A third cultural form that generated and mobilised groupings of active carnivalists was the masque band. The masquerade, or 'playing mas', was the central cultural form of the carnival. Changing one's everyday role and assuming a different one is another way of seeking release from the constraints of ordinary daily life, and a large number of people attended the carnival in a disguise of some sort whether or not they had an 'official' masquerade role.

A real masquerade is a group activity, which is planned and carefully organised and choreographed by artists. The group thus formed, referred to as a 'mas band' or 'costume band', gathers together regularly for several months to prepare for their appearance and performance on the carnival days. They debate about the theatrical theme which they will enact, hold frequent parties to gather more people to their ranks, study the designs worked out for the theme so that each member may register for the role she or he will play and for the costume that goes with it. They participate in costume-making by attending at the 'mas camp' during the weeks leading to the big event. Eventually they try the costumes on and rehearse the theatricality of the theme, accompanied by the steel band or sound system with which they will appear in the parade. Each masquerader is assigned a position or section within the band as the theme requires. Finally they attend the precarnival gala, in which their 'King' and 'Queen' take part in a competition for the coveted titles of 'Queen of the Bands' and 'King of the Bands'. On carnival day they help one another adjust their costumes and take their positions within the band and relate to each other in accordance with the theatrical theme. Often they indirectly involve their spouses, parents, neighbours and friends some of whom serve as helpers and followers.

Throughout these activities the members meet frequently, dancing, drinking and eating together and engaging in endless informal discussions about funding, the police and the local authorities as well as about general social and cultural issues. In due course strong communal relationships are developed between them, which outlast the carnival and lead to genuine friendships.

The mas bands provided colour, glitter, brilliance and wonder to the carnival makers. They excited the imagination by their 'meanings'. Mas making is an art form in its own right that involves knowledge, skills, imagination and creativity. Designers must understand the human body and its movements in order to create costumes and masks that are comfortable to wear and flexible enough to exploit the body's natural movements in playing the roles. The players must dominate the costume, not be dominated by it. This was one of the reasons why players were encouraged to participate in making their own costumes. A heavy mask can seriously damage the neck or shoulders of a player. However, conventional designers did not always heed these technical points and went for bulky costumes that were so heavy that part of the weight was borne on wheels. (That was particularly the case with the costumes of queens and kings of the bands, which were created, designed and produced at great effort and expense, mainly for display on stage at the aforementioned competition in the gala performance on the eve of the carnival for the coveted prizes. Those masques were sometimes too delicate and cumbersome to display in the street procession. Designers also had to pay attention to the durability of the costumes which had to withstand many hours of vigorous movement, crowding and exposure to wind and possibly rain.

Mas bands differ in their artistry, subtlety of theme and the sophistication of their costumes. In 1980 a mas band with the title 'If you are not Red you are Dread' was hastily formed. The organisers explained that, as many West Indians had come from islands that had no carnival tradition, or simply did not want to go to the bother and expense of an elaborate masquerade, people could form a mas band by simply coming to the procession wearing red clothes, no matter what shape or design the clothes were. All that was planned was to prepare twelve girls wearing red miniskirts to head the procession. The band was advertised on the BBC Radio London 'Black Londoners' programme. A precarnival party was arranged and a fee of £2.00 was collected to pay for the music attending them. That was a very simple mas band. Most, if not all, the other costume bands were far more serious and elaborate in their themes and costumes, attending frequent meetings to prepare for the event. They were formed by clubs, island associations, steel bands, sound systems, neighbourhoods and church congregations. The choice of a theme was reached after long discussions at the band meetings. Consideration was given to colour, weight, cost, symbolic significance, theatricality.

During the 1970s a controversy arose among the mas designers, both in Trinidad and Notting Hill, about the theatrical potentialities of the carnival masquerade. It was brought about by the work of Peter Minshall, a Trinidadian artist who had studied at London's Central School of Art and Design and worked for a while as a designer for the British theatre. In 1975 he designed the theme 'Paradise Lost' for a band of two thousand masqueraders for the Trinidad Carnival. It was a supreme artistic achievement, was selected as 'Band of the Year' and described as 'Band of the Century'. 'Paradise Lost' had four major sections: Pandemonium, Eden, Paradise, Sin and Death. 'There were hell hounds and fallen angels, a tree of life and Archangel Gabriel, traditional jab molasses and jumbies'. Movement was built into their costumes, which were light and highly manoeuvrable, allowing the actors to move their bodies freely in accordance with their roles. Most stunning was the

King of the Band, the Serpent, whose costume was designed for a particular man to wear; his powerful physique was the centre of a vast leaf attached to his ankles and thighs; when he danced in that costume he simply blazed. In the next few years Minshall designed more masquerades in Trinidad and one ('Skytribe') in Notting Hill, then accepted a Professorship of Drama in an American college.[5]

Mas design has never been the same again, whether in Trinidad or in Notting Hill. The traditional designers were at first stunned, then began to argue that Minshall's work was more suitable for the theatre than for a street carnival. Nevertheless, their subsequent work showed his influence on carnival mas, which was often described as 'theatre of the street'.

However, in the Notting Hill Carnival, mas as theatre remained an ideal to be realised. Probably the strictly traditional form of theatre did not fit the occasion. In both Trinidad and Notting Hill mas had been evolved as a distinct form of art in its own right, with its own conventions. The highly elaborate and often enigmatic masques of the Kings and Queens of bands are like the masks of West Africa, whose exaggerated features were not the result of 'primitive' artistry or irrational design but were created as a thought-provoking image. Similarly, just as the West African carver worked in ritual secrecy and prohibited any commoners from seeing the mask in the making, so did the carnival mas artist producing the King and Queen of the Band costumes work in secrecy. Ostensibly this was to keep competitors from other bands in the dark, but largely, and perhaps unconsciously, to prevent the audience from seeing the unfinished masque in the process of construction from elementary materials, thus maximising the dramatic impact of the accomplished mask when it was finally unveiled for the public.

Over the years, mas in Notting Hill ranged over hundreds of themes, within broad categories, that were both meaningful and exotic: African, Caribbean, European, biblical, historical, maritime, cosmological and mythological; forests, birds, butterflies, space travel, rainbows and nature fantasies also featured. Some themes recurred more frequently than others. Thus 'Ancient Egypt' was a particularly popular theme because it was both exotic and symbolically significant, displaying a sophisticated African civilisation.

5. See the *Observer*, 19 Aug. 1979.

(Many West Indians believed that Africa was the cradle of human civilisation and that white historians had deliberately suppressed that fact.) Another theme was related to Amerindians, and was, again, a popular choice both for its colour and exotic masques and the idelological twist which emphasised their struggle against white domination.

Mas designers distinguish between 'pretty mas' and 'serious mas', saying that the most successful mas was one that combined the two. The mas band Lion Youth started their deliberation over their mas theme one year with an initial decision that it should be 'Birds'. That had been a frequently chosen subject for a typically pretty mas, but they spent many sessions discussing how to transform it to convey a serious message too. They considered calling it 'Wings of Liberation', but finally settled for 'Wings of Freedom'.

A few mas bands played the same theme year after year. Grenadan Shortney, for instance, played the same traditional mas, using the same costumes, chanting without musical instruments as they paraded and throwing talcum powder over people each year. This was a 'traditional' mas that had originated in the post-slavery era when many of the costumes were chosen to parody white people.

The steel bands, mas bands and sound systems that the carnival needed, and, in fact, generated, developed and maintained a vast network of interpersonal relations the ramifications of which spread throughout the West Indian community. The lives of different bands and sound systems involved cultural activities that led their members, supporters and followers to interact intensively for many months during which time they ate, smoked and talked together. In the course of their interaction they informally discussed carnival affairs: finances, policing and relations with the residents and with the local authorities. They also gossiped and discussed the internal politics of the carnival: the organising committee, the various levels of leadership and the different associations and factions involved. Inevitably, they discussed major political issues concerning the West Indian community generally, its internal and external politics. Thus politics was built into interpersonal relationships and became rooted in the psyche of the people involved.

Through interaction between bands in a variety of situations, different band and sound system networks became interconnected. They were further linked by their involvement with the organising committee and in the leadership process generally. In due course the networks of the various groupings at different levels overlapped and cut across each other, and if we superimpose on these networks those of the numerous primary neighbourhood groupings, island of origin groupings, church and Rastafarian groupings, as well as the complex network of kinship and affinity, we find that what had evolved was a colossal corporate network of communication which reached almost the whole West Indian community in the country.

This major network, in its whole and in parts, outlasted the annual carnival and assumed an existence in its own right quite apart from the carnival. It served as a system of communication between the various parts of the community, making it possible for them to exchange information, discuss general political problems and strategies, deliberate and accumulate experience. It was a fairly enduring network.

It is clear from the above discussion that steel band music, the sound system, and the masquerade are popular grassroots cultural forms which catered for the masses. The Notting Hill Carnival did not invent them, but mobilised, modified and adjusted them to contemporary conditions in Britain. This is not a return to the past or the simple continuity of traditional forms but a manipulation of these forms to deal with the present.

8

The Leadership Process

The articulation of a rational corporate political organisation in terms of non-rational cultural forms and dramaturgical techniques though achieved mainly through the leadership process is essentially a collective endeavour. Through communication the collectivity becomes aware of its on-going problems, loosely deliberate them and probe for solutions. As its members differ in age, sex, experience, training, interests, abilities and intellect, they stimulate one another and in the process some of them prove to be more perceptive, more creative, more original than others in tackling one or another of the current corporate issues and thus are thrown up as leaders. These are not necessarily charismatic men or women, nor are they fully conscious of their role. As we are dealing here essentially with communal politics, where cultural forms and political formations are dynamically interconnected, leadership is inevitably ambiguous, being partly rational and partly non-rational, partly conscious and partly non-conscious, partly intentional and partly non-intentional.

Frank Crichlow, from 1969 to 1991 owner of the Mangrove, was not a 'leader' in any *formal* sense. He was shy, diffident, not a distinguished speaker. He never sought any important formal position in the community, nor did he harbour any pretensions of being a leader of any kind, nor did he possess any distinct charismatic traits. Yet, in effect, he had been – he continues to be at the time of writing – one of the most significant West Indian leaders in Britain during the 1970s and 1980s. His role in the development of the Notting Hill Carnival was paramount.

He came to Britain in the early 1950s and after a short period of work in one or two jobs he opened a restaurant-cafe, the Rio. He reckoned at the time that the West Indians in that part of London needed a meeting place where they felt at home and relaxed from the pressures of white society. They were lonely individuals away from their families, mainly males, and often with no permanent place of residence. From the very start he stressed that his establishment would bring together West Indians from all the different islands of origin.

After a short time the Rio became associated with gambling, drinking and drug taking. In 1969 he opened the Mangrove in All Saints Road and shortly afterwards closed the Rio. The Mangrove catered at that time to local white as well as black residents, and was indeed eagerly patronised by some of the bohemian artists, writers, students and hippies who had been living in the area.

Crichlow was a musician and over the years the Mangrove was frequented by other musicians. For well over a decade his restaurant/club/wine bar/community centre was the carnival nerve centre where ideas were discussed, action planned and decisions taken. He helped in the development of steel bands, for many years holding his own 'Panorama' competition between them, with a special panel of judges on his premises to choose the winners of prizes he personally donated. On carnival days sound systems took it in turn to play for him, and All Saints Road was always dense with thousands of revellers.

This road of feverish jollity was also the most important centre for drug pushers, and was sometimes described by the media as the most heavily policed street in Europe. Crichlow was unavoidably affected in a variety of ways by this. It was common knowledge that a large number of West Indian men smoked marijuana, the Rastafarian among them maintaining that they did so on religious grounds. This is a mild, relatively cheap drug and some experts even argue that it is harmless and that it ought not be proscribed by law. The police were aware that smoking it was part of West Indian life style and, although its consumption was arrestable and could theoretically lead to imprisonment, they generally turned a blind eye to those who smoked it, particularly as they would otherwise involve themselves in further problems, though their attitude about the drug suppliers and pushers was less tolerant. Possibly the existence of networks of marijuana trafficking encouraged dealing in more serious drugs which the police could not neglect.

Thus, from its inception, the Mangrove became the target of continuous raids by the police and that led to the fierce confrontation between West Indian demonstrators and the police in 1970.[1]

1. See Chapter 2 above.

That incident, and the long trial that followed it, became a milestone, as it raised the whole problem of race relations in Britain. Police raids on the Mangrove continued throughout the 1970s and 1980s. Some of those raids led to Crichlow's arrest. (He himself estimated that he had been arrested about 50 times since he came to Britain.) He never gave up, though, and over those years he provided other services for the community. In particular he became a refuge for young West Indians released from prison, offering them advice as well as material help. In this way, a large number of men came, over the years, to owe him allegiance. When the Mangrove was raided by the police, many of these men rushed to his aid, ready to do anything in his defence. It is ironic that the police at times called on him for help and advice with the youths, even though they regarded him as a suspect criminal whom they had brought to court on various charges at different times.

Perhaps one of the most bizarre revelations in a typical court case was that his photograph had been pinned on the wall of the local police station. In September 1979, one week after the carnival, two plain-clothed police officers chased a white woman suspect who, on seeing them had run into the Mangrove. When they entered after her their way was blocked by six black men. At the same time about thirty more men rushed to the scene, among them Crichlow. One of the two officers started arguing that he was a police officer and persisted in entering the restaurant, but his colleague whispered to him words to the effect that if he went in he would be a dead man. They retreated and called for help. Within a few minutes several police cars with fifty officers appeared in front of the restaurant and commotion broke out. Crichlow was arrested and eventually brought to a magistrate's court. The police alleged that he had been waving a screwdriver in the air in a very excited state shouting: 'Let us kill these fucking pigs once and for all . . . Let us do what we should have done last week' (meaning during the last carnival). The counsel for the defence asked the police officer who had led the force how he identified Crichlow from among the crowd. The officer said he had seen his photograph on the wall at Notting Hill police station. Why was the photograph pinned on the wall? For playing darts with? After many evasive statements the officer said: 'Because he is a known criminal'. Later in the trial another police officer tried to rectify the situation by telling the court that Crichlow's photograph was one of many other photographs on the wall, not just of criminals but also of others, including local councillors as well as a judge. The defence pointed out the long-term cooperation Crichlow had given the police in mediation with the black community and the fact that he had been given a special telephone number by the police commander so that he could ring him in cases of trouble. The defence wanted to call four or five more witnesses but the magistrate halted the trial and said he wanted to hear no more. He dismissed the charges, saying that the credibility of some police witnesses was in question.[2]

As the 1980s rolled on, as rapid gentrification of the area brought an increasing number of 'yuppies' as new residents, as the police fight against drug trafficking intensified and as the carnival expanded and almost hit the two million mark in attendance, police pressure on Crichlow and his Mangrove became almost overwhelming.

What looked like a showdown occurred in mid-1988, when he was arrested on serious drug charges, only to be acquitted in a stormy trial over a year later.[3] Five days after his acquittal he convened a meeting of the Mangrove Community Association at which it was decided to oppose the 'collaborators' Carnival' (i.e. the one organised by the new committee, the CEC), by staging their own carnival in All Saints Road in the same area. Other community leaders intervened, though, and persuaded Crichlow and his associates to avoid a split in the community by refraining from staging a rival carnival, promising to debate the situation in public when the impending carnival was over.

What was astonishing about Crichlow was that he did not give up. During twenty turbulent years he made the Mangrove into a potent symbol of black unity, defiance and resistance. For the carnival, he was in fact a 'guardian of the stage', providing a constant territorial base for an otherwise precariously poised, perennially threatened celebration. Throughout most of its existence the carnival had had no permanent, continuously manned office. The Mangrove was a substitute, serving as a centre of communication, as a permanent address. (Darcus Howe: 'The Mangrove is my permanent link with Notting Hill'.) In this way, by making the Mangrove into an informal information centre as well as a meeting place for them Crichlow made it possible for artists, musicians, organisers and political activists, to communicate and meet. He was ideologically committed to help unify the heterogeneous

2. See *KN*, 21 Dec. l979 and 28 Dec. 1979.
3. See Chapter 5 above.

islanders within a common identity. He also mediated between the generations by bringing together young and old. Without any conscious endeavour he acquired through his services to the community a high degree of moral authority, which he duly exercised in different situations.

A different type of leadership, more direct, calculated and conscious was provided by Darcus Howe – political activist, committed carnivalist, ideologist, organiser, articulate speaker, writer. The carnival became politically and culturally radical under his influence and he left an enduring mark on its structure.

He was a close friend of Crichlow and a permanent associate of the Mangrove community and of the many pioneering steelbands men, mas men and sound system men who frequented it. He was the leading figure among the Mangrove Nine who played an active role in the organisation of the 1970 demonstration and turned the long trial that followed it from a tedious court case to a drama of protest. At the time he was an active member of the Black Panther Movement based in Brixton, where he lived. He led a busy life as chairman of the Race Today Collective and editor of its journal from 1974, operating on national and international scales.

He had been steeped in the steelband movement since his early childhood in Trinidad, where he was a member of a well-known band called Renegades, of East Dry River, Port of Spain. He even managed to become involved in youth gang warfare, to be arrested and imprisoned. He eventually became an honorary life-member of the same band. Steelband music was in his blood, he told me in an interview.

He came to Britain in 1962, aged 18. He participated in the Notting Hill Carnival from its early years and in 1976 was elected chairman of the Carnival Development Committee (CDC). He had already been writing about the carnival in the pages of the journal *Race Today*, since he had become its editor. In articles and speeches over the years he developed what amounted to a politico-cultural ideology of carnival, that helped in a big way to transform the structure of the London event. Some of those statements became major slogans in the movement and part of its mythology. For example, in an article in *Race Today* he described Notting Hill as 'the closest to being liberated territory',[4] referring to the resistance to and counter attack against white racists who had assaulted

4. *Race Today*, Oct. 1974.

the West Indians in the area during the 1958 race riots. He was resolved that 'Carnival will for ever be held on the streets of Notting Hill',[5] while another slogan stated: 'We have captured the streets of Notting Hill and transformed it into an arena of cultural rebellion'.[6] Those slogans solidified the determination of the carnival makers in later years in their stand in the face of mounting pressure to remove the carnival to a different venue. When it was suggested that the carnival should be confined to a stadium he retorted with a quotation from the Trinidad calypsonian Lord Kitchener which he used as a title of a *Race Today* booklet on carnival: *The Road Make to Walk on Carnival Day*. He wrote: 'The staging of Carnival on the streets of Notting Hill is a political victory'.[7]

He regarded Carnival as a cultural rebellion against the dominant British culture which, he argued, was being imposed on the West Indians. He said :'The struggle for culture is a struggle for authenticity', and said that rather than accepting the dictates of the dominant culture, the West Indians were overlaying their own cultural forms on that culture. 'Our festivals and artifacts', he said, 'are fast becoming public forms in these islands – as indigenous as yorkshire pudding'.[8] He fully appreciated the political potentialities of the carnival, though he insisted all the time that the celebration was essentially a cultural, artistic event and should be developed and cultivated as such, not only in order to deny the authorities the excuse to ban it, but also, paradoxically, to make it politically more efficacious. He dwelt on the importance of 'educating the public' – meaning essentially West Indians from islands that had no carnival tradition as well as those who were born in Britain – about the history, arts and political significance of the festival.

As a writer, journalist and political activist he focused on the police and was thus always in the forefront of the politics of racism in Britain. He organised protest marches and demonstrations, exposed police malpractice and harassment in their dealings with the black community and addressed public opinion, not only in Britain but also in North America and the Caribbean, mobilising in the process the support of the extensive black diaspora. 'We have shattered the myth of the nice British bobby' he wrote.[9] His rage

5. *Race Today*, Jan. 1978:8.
6. *Race Today*, Sept.–Oct. 1978.
7. *Race Today*, Sept. 1976.
8. *Race Today*, Jan. 1978.
9. For a collection of his writing on the police see D. Howe, *From Bobby to Babylon: Blacks and the British Police*, London, Race Today Publications, 1988.

against the police was at times expressed in violent terms as is illustrated in his account of the 1970 Mangrove clash with the police: 'We gave them as good as we got. Bricks, stones, bottles, any ammunition at hand, we threw at the police. Whole building skips were emptied at them'.[10]

He not only wrote and lectured on Carnival and on politics but also practised what he preached, taking part in events in person. In the carnival he sometimes played in a steel band and sometimes in a mas band. In 1978 he not only served as chairman of the Carnival Development Committee but also organised and led a mas band into which he had drawn hundreds of youths from Brixton and which he characteristically called '*Race Today* Mangrove Renegade Band', which enacted a theme called 'Forces of victory'. In 1982 he organised and led a march of over ten thousand people called 'Black People Day of Action'. It started from the East End of London and ended in the West End, protesting against an alleged police 'cover up' of the identity of white racists, whom, it was assumed by the marchers, had started a fire that killed thirteen black youths who had been celebrating a birthday in a private house.[11]

A deep sense of passionate outrage against racial discrimination inspired Howe's personal impulse to action. He spoke, wrote and acted with deep emotion. In 1977 a judge described him as 'touchy and arrogant' and sentenced him to three months in prison for quarrelling with a white ticket collector in Notting Hill underground station who had called him a 'black cunt'. (A well-organised national and international campaign expressed in telegrams, petitions and demonstrations, demanding his immediate release succeeded in freeing him after a week.)

Howe, then, was an activist on the two main fronts of culture and politics; the two types of endeavour deeply rooted in his personality, biography and network of interpersonal relationships. He brought both to bear on the struggle of the West Indians within the British polity. For him the carnival was only one of the arenas in which he operated. Thus, although he was chairman of the CDC he left much of the local Notting Hill affairs to the then director of CDC, Selwyn Baptiste.

Baptiste was born and brought up in a rural area in Trinidad

10. Howe,*Babylon*, p.44.
11. See Howe *Babylon*.

and came to Britain in 1960, aged 18. He had already had a great deal of experience in steelband music when in 1966 he was commissioned to form a steel band for youths in a playground in Notting Hill. He, together with the youths made the pans which he tuned himself. He was soon asked by Rhaune Laslett to play in the forthcoming 1967 carnival. Already, for the first carnival, in 1966, Russ Henderson had formed a small band of three players who continued to take part for many years afterwards. Henderson was essentially a professional pianist, though, and played steelband music mainly during carnival. Baptiste's band, on the other hand, became the first established band and over the years evolved into one of the most important steel bands in Britain, the Metronomes. After the success of his band in the 1967 carnival, Baptiste assumed a growing importance in the carnival movement. In the wake of the stormy 1976 carnival, he was asked by the steelband men, the mas men and the sound system men, who formed the new CDC, to act as director. He was, in fact, one of them, both as musician and as a friend. He had spent long evenings with them, drinking, smoking and chatting. He knew them well personally and felt with them the problems they confronted.

He jealously developed and guarded the West Indian character of the celebration and discouraged the incursion of 'foreign' cultural forms into its structure. In an interview with *Race Today* he indicated that from the start, during the first few years of the carnival when it was multicultural in its arts and music and multi-ethnic in attendance, and was referred to as a fair, he strived to turn it into an exclusively West Indian celebration, to 'purify' it of the contamination of native British cultural forms:

> They saw this thing developing to a great extent and wanted to change the character of it. I wouldn't move or budge an inch. For example they wanted to give the Carnival a different name. . . They were also trying to involve the host community in a dominant way by bringing in bagpipes and all different things which would water down the West Indian character.[12]

He even dismissed the slogan that the carnival existed to bring whites and blacks together. He said: 'We are no race relations industry . . . Carnival is a cultural, not a political event'.[13]

He was certainly exaggerating the efficacy of his role in chang-

12. Sept.–Oct, 1977, p.141.
13. Interview, 'Black Londoners'.

ing the character of the event, because there were other factors involved in the eventual change. However, he was expressing a sociologically significant issue: that there was at the time a sustained, conscious effort to establish cultural and social boundaries, to achieve a distinctiveness that would mark the identity and exclusiveness that would be necessary for the articulation of a corporate West Indian organisation. Indeed, his West Indian critics in later years accused him of harbouring narrow 'island nationalism' by systematically upholding the Trinidadian stamp over the event. The local paper *Grassroots* castigated him over that.[14]

Like most other West Indian men, he had his share of discrimination and the inevitable encounter with the police. In 1969 he went to a club in the company of six white friends, only to be asked to leave because he was black.[15] In 1978, when he was at the height of his power and authority in the carnival movement as director of the CDC, he was brought to a magistrate's court for allegedly shouting at the police who had stopped the car in which he was travelling at about four o'clock in the morning. The police claimed that he had threatened them saying: 'We will kill all of you fuckers at Notting Hill this year'. The defence Counsel alleged police conspiracy, but the court found him guilty and fined him £20 with £50 costs.[16]

Baptiste was not a politician, but his contribution to distinctiveness in terms of cultural exclusiveness, was politically significant. However, the development of unity, identity and collective consciousness are not by themselves sufficient to create a functioning political organisation. It is also essential to develop a system of communication among members, particularly if those members were scattered in different neighbourhoods within a vast, complex city like London. Among the West Indians a great deal of communication was conducted through parties, religious gatherings, clubs, sound systems and pirate local radio stations.

Far more effective than anything else, though, was the carnival movement and its institutional ramifications. Many people contributed to this: a significant role being played by Alex Pascall who served as chairman of the CAC from 1984 to 1989. Pascall sometimes acted as adviser to the Arts Council on Afro-Caribbean music, sometimes as vice-president of the Foundation of European

14. *Grassroots*, Aug.–Sept. 1977.
15. See *KP*, 14 Feb., 1969.
16. For details see *West London Observer*, 6 April 1978.

Carnival Cities. He was known nationally and internationally as a man of many talents: singer, songwriter, percussionist, disc jockey, master of ceremonies, writer, story teller. For about 15 years he produced and presented, often single-handedly, the daily BBC radio programme 'Black Londoners' in which over the years he interviewed almost every Afro-Caribbean artist, musician and writer in Britain. Although born in Grenada, where no significant carnival tradition existed, he had adopted the Notting Hill Carnival as 'our heritage', patronised, monitored and celebrated it from the very beginning, providing extensive news and features about it throughout each year, interviewing carnival organisers, artists and musicians, police and grant givers. The BBC did not engage in commercial advertising, but Pascall managed to keep his programme wide open for broadcasting announcements and news from hundreds of West Indian clubs and associations about meetings, parties and concerts – all free of charge.

On Carnival Sunday and Monday he spent many hours in Notting Hill, accompanied by a mobile studio, cameramen and engineers. Reporters positioned in different parts of the area covered the comings and goings in the celebration, describing what was going on and interviewing carnival makers in the streets, all in a live broadcast on Radio London. Pascall was truly 'the Great Communicator' for the West Indians in London; a community that was scattered in different parts of the metropolis, in which travel from one part to another took a long time and was prohibitively expensive for poor people.

In his radio programme, Pascall alternated talks and interviews with music, particularly reggae, soca and calypso and that attracted even the youths to listen to the programme.

He also conducted live debates on the air, over the telephone as well as in the studio, about different topics and programmes, thus providing opportunities for scores of listeners at a time to express their views, to complain and criticise and to air different problems.

Although he was not renowned for ideological consistency, he displayed strong convictions and commitments in the carnival movement. 'Carnival', he said, 'has its historical cultural significance. Without culture we are nothing. You lose your identity and people do not know from where you came'.[17] Again, 'Carnival is our cultural identity . . . There is nothing in the United Kingdom that has the same flavour'.[18]

17. In a broadcast chat on 15 July 1984.
18. Chat on 3 Aug. 1984.

The few leaders mentioned so far, and many others, affected the political structure of the carnival, displaying, to a smaller or larger extent, an element of rational choice which in its turn was injected into the movement and changed its course. However, for the overwhelming majority of the carnival makers the intervention became part of the cultural 'tradition' of the celebration. But the change they brought about was not the whimsical invention of individuals. The leaders were themselves led by the collective, through intensive grass-roots interaction with them, to the type of innovation that emerged at the time. It was then that the originality, creativity and rationality of each individual leader came into its own.

To demonstrate this point I refer to a negative instance, to a highly qualified and gifted West Indian who aspired to become a carnival leader, but was eventually squeezed out by the movement. The reference is to Louis Chase, who became chairman of the CAC in 1978 and had to resign from his position a few months later.

Louis Chase was born in Barbados and came to Britain in 1960, aged 17. He was intelligent, highly educated, widely-read a free-lance writer, a lay Christian preacher. He was elegantly dressed all the time in a suit and a tie, spoke English with a flawless Oxford accent, was courteous and refined in his manners. He was so impressive a figure that *The Times* published a profile of him, including an elaborate artist's impression of his image, under the title 'The Black Man's Burden'.[19] All his gentlemanly appearance and conduct had not saved him from police harassment, though: he had been stopped, searched and abused on a number of occasions and was arrested and convicted by the courts for allegedly obstructing a police officer. He wrote once: 'All my life I have only wanted to be treated as a human being. Nothing more, nothing less'.[20]

He was deeply interested in politics and his central ambition was eventually to become a Labour member of parliament. He lived in Notting Hill, and saw the carnival as a political demonstration which was, as he repeatedly put it in his articles, sermons and speeches and in discussion: 'the only stage on which the youngsters act out the drama of their life'. He saw in the carnival a chance both to serve the community and advance his own career in politics. Although he came from a country that had no carnival tradition and he himself had no previous involvement in music or mas, he wrote

19. *The Times*, 30 Jan. 1978.
20. L. Chase, *Streets of Chance: The Future of Multicultural Society*, London, private publication, 1979.

at this time that: 'Carnival is our major expression of public dignity and it is for this reason that we continue the battle for its survival. . . . It is an occasion for the refurbishment of our identity with our Caribbean roots'.[21] In May 1978 in a Sunday church service to which he had invited me I heard him say in his sermon that the West Indians saw in the carnival an expression of their oppression as well as of their emancipation. He continued: 'Because of discrimination, injustice, and inequality, the Black community should fall back on its own historic and cultural resources in the dark beauty of African civilisation. This is necessary for its survival, self esteem. . . . Black people are spiritual people. . . . There is a need for a Third Testament for the Black community'.[22]

He had no sentimental roots in the community, however. He tended to be a loner. He had no followers to lead him. His brazen statements to the effect that the carnival was a political demonstration, alienated him from the musicians and artists. He had no clear programme to indicate how to run the carnival as a political demonstration. He was an excellent speaker, but not an orator who could inspire and rouse the masses. Too intelligent not to realise very quickly that he had no popular support he said so in public when he announced his resignation from the chairmanship of the CAC.

Not all leaders operated on the levels of collective organisation. In a communalist organisation, the leadership process operates through chains and hierarchies of leaders of different types in different fields of activity, on different levels of organisation, mostly in face to face interaction with followers. The managers, disc jockeys and toasters of the sound systems played fundamental roles in reflecting as well as shaping the views, interests, loyalties and sentiments of their massive young audiences. They regularly disseminated current carnival news, commented on it and, when relevant, proposed action. They were leaders in their own right. In such a way the La Rose brothers, Keith and Michael, of Finsbury Park, for many years wielded a great deal of influence over the youth of Finsbury Park and beyond, through their sound system, Peoples War.[23] They were in the forefront of a new type of West Indian leadership, highly educated, well-informed, committed.

21. See L. Chase, *Notting Hill Carnival – Street Festival*, London, private publication, 1978.
22. L. Chase, London, *The Power and the Glory*, private publication, 1978.
23. See details in Chapter 4.

Michael La Rose became manager of New Beacon Books and was for some time vice-chairman of the CDC. He was also associated with Black Youth Movement, Black Students Association and Black Parents Association, of which his father was the president. Through his partnership in the Peoples War sound system and his position as coordinator of the Peoples War Carnival Band he kept continuous contacts with the youths of the area. At the same time through his position in New Beacon Books he was in contact with many black intellectuals. Although the La Roses were originally Trinidadians, and were probably expected to be active in the steelband and calypso-type music, they crossed the island divide and adopted the Jamaican-style sound system, initially playing mainly reggae music. Their contribution to the Notting Hill Carnival movement was immense. They organised mas bands and were among the pioneers who put sound systems on wheels to become part of the mobile section of the carnival. They linked the Finsbury Park grass-roots carnival makers to the centre of the carnival movement by serving as members in the Carnival Development Committee and by continual meetings with other leaders and artists from other areas of London. They thus combined art and politics to educate as well as to guide youth forces in the Finsbury Park area and to mediate between them and the levels of leadership.

In the wake of the highly restricted carnival of 1989, Michael La Rose initiated and led significant meetings of leading carnival makers and representatives of bands to discuss police pressure and domination of the carnival. He eventually edited and published two booklets on the proceedings.[24] He was elected chairman of the newly formed Notting Hill International Carnival Committee.

On yet another level in the leadership process, Betty and Leslie, the initial organisers of Lion Youth in the 1977 carnival, were leaders in their own way. They were highly inventive, for they went beyond the conventional carnival to express and guide the mood of West Indian youth in the late 1970s in terms of a new artistic-political move. Leslie Wills, for many years a committed carnivalist and youth leader, repeatedly emphasised during numerous interviews that, although she had been brought up in Guiana, carnival was in her blood. She emphasised the fact that she had been born in Notting Hill, in a house in All Saints Road opposite the Mangrove Restaurant, before her family took her to Guiana. She eventually

24. See M. La Rose, *Mas in Notting Hill*, London, New Beacon Books, 1990.

graduated from the North London Art College and worked for a time as a designer for Larry Forde's Sukuya Mas Band. The dissertation for her finals was on the Notting Hill Carnival. She lived in Finsbury Park and was in close contact with the youths of the area as well as with the local intellectuals. Her mother taught African dancing at the Commonwealth Institute.

Again, Malcolm Thomas, who had nothing to do with the carnival back home in Trinidad, experienced, after only one year in Britain, a compelling urge to express his identity in steelband music and, later, to help others by applying his organisational skills to utilise talents, ideas and personnel for the Ebony Steel and Mas Band. What these few sketches show is that leadership is a collective process in which all members of the collectivity are involved, each contributing to the corporation their experience and specialised effort, all the time bringing political and cultural factors to bear on one another. In this process rational political strategies inform and transform non-rational cultural forms. Leadership is not essentially a matter of charisma or of special individual qualifications. Communal leaders have no tenure of office. The situation is dynamic; circumstances change continuously and new styles, ideas, abilities that could be provided by other personnel may accordingly be required.[25]

25. For a general discussion of communal leadership in Britain see M. Anwar, *The Context of Leadership*, and P. Werbner, 'Black and Ethnic Leadership in Britain', in M. Anwar and P. Werbner (eds.) *Blacks and Ethnic Leadership*, London and New York, Routledge, 1991.

9

The Politics of Joking
Relationships

Culture and politics were dynamically related in the development and structure of the carnival, but the event, like all other
symbolic forms, is not reducible to either. It is a multivocal form,
an ambiguous unity of political and cultural significance, combining the rational and the non-rational, the conscious and the non-
conscious.

Despite the crucial part played by politics in shaping the structure of the cultural event, it is futile to try to explain, or explain
away, the cultural in terms of the political. Indeed, cultural symbols and the communal relationships they express and sustain are
so powerful in their hold on people that political formations everywhere, including the state, always attempt to manipulate them in
their own interests. This is a fundamental analytical issue, but
instead of discussing it in abstract terms, I shall deal with it here by
examining a serious rift in the carnival leadership in the wake of the
1976 violent encounter between the police and West Indian youth.
The rift resulted in the formation of two rival committees, the
Carnival Development Committee (CDC) and the Carnival and
Arts Committee (CAC). Many issues were involved in that split-
financial, personal, island-of-origin loyalties, neighbourhood – but
by far the most basic was the question of whether the carnival was
essentially a political or a cultural movement.[1]

The CAC combined two streams of thought the general orientation of which can be described as utilitarian. The first was represented by Louis Chase,[2] for a brief period CAC's chairman, who

1. The split into two committees was discussed extensively in the press at the
time. See *Westindian World* 11, 18, and 25 Feb. 1977; D. Howe, *The Road Make
to Walk on Carnival Day*, London, Race Today Publications, 1977; L. Chase,
Notting Hill Carnival – Street Festival, London, private publication, 1978.

argued that the carnival was essentially a political event and should be used as a political weapon to press for reforms and concessions. When his critics charged that he knew nothing about carnival traditions and conventions, he retorted that the coal miners' leaders in Britain were not always coal miners themselves. His stance was generally supported by four local black organisations on the committee. The second stream of thought within the CAC was commercially inclined, arguing that the carnival held immense economic possibilities for West Indians, that it could be promoted as a tourist attraction and made into a base for related industries, producing, for example, special T-shirts, costumes and masks, thereby providing employment for members of the community.

Until 1976, those leaders were part of one unified carnival committee. Their views, however, were rejected by other members of the original committee, most particularly by the leading artists in the steel and mas bands and the calypsonians, who eventually quit the committee and reestablished themselves as the Carnival Development Committee (CDC), proclaiming that *they* were the carnival, that there could be no carnival without them.

The CDC artists and organisers were no less politically or financially conscious than the CAC, but they argued that the carnival was essentially an artistic, creative event *sui generis*, of value in its own right, and that any overt, instrumental exploitation of it would destroy it altogether, would in fact nullify its political impact. They implied that only if it were overtly nonpolitical could it be politically effective. The journal *Race Today* published a long letter to the editor signed by a Rastaman, Dread Ray, in which he declared that turning the carnival into a political protest was a sure way of destroying it; that he did not go to carnival to demonstrate, but to 'enjoy I self in love and unity with I people'.[3] Larry Forde, sometimes mas officer as well as secretary of the CDC, expressed sorrow when, in the 1977 carnival, a radical political party entered a float bedecked with placards saying 'the police are the muggers'; he himself was probably no less antagonised by the police, but he argued that that kind of slogan did not fit the nature of the event, that the same message could in fact have been conveyed indirectly in an artistic form, probably with greater effect. The CDC Chairman at the time was Darcus Howe, one of the most radical political activists among the West Indians in Britain, but he maintained that without any overt political message, the very fact that

3. Jul.–Aug. 1977:115.

hundreds of thousands of people came to Notting Hill to attend the carnival in the face of continued opposition from the police, the local council and some local residents and in the face of internal factionalism, that fact alone was a political event of the first order. The CDC was not unaware of the importance of finance but maintained that, once it commercialised the carnival, its arts would become pecuniary arts and various carnival groups would end up becoming instrumental parts of the hegemony of the established system. The committee did seek financial aid from public institutions, particularly from the Arts Council, but insisted on having no strings attached. They said they were not begging but demanding grants by right as tax-paying citizens. At the same time they attempted to raise money from the proceeds of pre-carnival public performances by various bands so as not to rely on 'the handouts of the state and other charitable trusts'.[4] The general view of artists and organisers in the CDC, then, was that the carnival was first and foremost a cultural event and that, once it was directly politicised, its essential character would change and the masses would no longer participate, leaving on the road only political activists who would inevitably transform it into a political demonstration.

This cleavage between the two committees should not be exaggerated. The CDC had some politicians and the CAC had some artists and the same men often combined concern with both sides. The controversy was very much a manifestation of the growth and increasing complexity of the carnival movement. A similar debate could be found within the Rastafarian movement and also within the Black Power movement in the United States. The issue was paramount, for example in the work of the black American poet and dramatist Amiri Baraka, who pointed out that all writers have their political line, but that the question is *how* to express that artistically without descending to propaganda.[5] The black British poet and writer Linton Kwesi Johnson put the problem differently: 'If politics creeps into art unconsciously, without the writer trying, that is often the most powerful political expression; but when artists try to be political in their art, it usually ends up badly, whether in poetry or in a novel or other art forms. People do not like to be preached at'.[6]

The same issue was raised by the dramatist Bertolt Brecht, who

4. *Westindian World*, 18 May 1979.
5. See W. Sollors, *Amiri Basaka Solidus Le Roi Jones*, New York, Columbia University Press, 1978, pp.251–3.
6. *Race Today*, Feb. 1977.

directed a polemic against so-called socialist realism which, during Stalin's reign in the USSR, ended up in crude glorification of the revolution, the party and its leaders. The inherent lack of subtlety in socialist realism left the Soviet theatre of the time playing to nearly empty houses.[7] Brecht maintained that a truly Marxist theatre should aim at making the audience think for themselves, actively and creatively. Another writer, Herbert Marcuse, reverted to 'two-dimensionality' attributing autonomy to art.[8] Along the same line of thought, Irving Howe concluded his argument in *Politics and the Novel* stating that: 'At its best, the political novel generates such intense heat that the political ideas it appropriates are melted into its movement and fused with the emotions of its characters'.[9]

This issue of the nature of the relation between art and politics is part of the broader question of the relation between culture and power, which for many decades now has been the central concern of both marxist and bourgeois intellectuals, and is also the central problematic of social anthropology. Thus, in a survey of Western Marxism, Perry Anderson, editor of *New Left Review*, states that Western Marxism as a whole, when it proceeds beyond questions of method to matters of substance, comes to concentrate overwhelmingly on the study of superstructure in relation to power structure.[10] This is evident in Gramsci, Althusser, Marcuse, Sartre, and the literally hundreds of publications on ideology and on Marxian approaches to literature, art and philosophy. One of Britain's most distinguished and prolific academic Marxists, Raymond Williams, devoted his career to exploring this problematic and the *New Left Review* published a large volume entitled *Raymond Williams, Politics and Letters*, based on a series of extensive interview sessions conducted with Williams by three members of the editorial board, all of which deal with the relations between culture and politics.[11] Anderson concludes his survey by saying that Western Marxism had 'achieved a sophistication greater than that of any previous phase of historical materialism'.[12]

Similarly, mainline Western 'bourgeois' social science has focused on this problematic in various ways, dealing with the role of culture in the maintenance of the power structure, essentially appre-

7. M. Esslin, *Brecht's Choice of Evils*, London, Heinemann, 1977.
8. H. Marcuse, *The Aesthetic Dimension*, London, Macmillan, 1979.
9. I. Howe, *Politics and the Novel*, Cleveland, Meridian, 1957, p.21.
10. P. Anderson, *Considerations on Western Marxism*, London, NLB,. 1976.
11. R. Williams, *Politics and Letters: Interviews with New Left Review*, London, Oxford University Press, 1979.
12. Anderson, *Western Marxism*.

hending the philosophical problem posed by Hobbes about the source and nature of social consensus in the maintenance of law and order. This line of thinking is evident in Weber and Durkheim and later in the functionalism of Parsons. Indeed, just as the Marxists assumed the existence of a dominant ideology incorporating the whole polity, so did Parsons and his followers conceive of a dominant common culture consisting of basic values, norms and beliefs shared among the members of society. The main difference between the two streams of thinking is that, while the marxists maintain that the dominant ideology is imposed by the ruling class on the subordinate classes, the Parsonians hold that the dominant culture is generated by consensus. It may be interesting to note in this connection that as early as the 1960s there was a great deal of interest in Parsonian functionalism among sociologists in the Soviet Union.[13] About a decade later some detailed reports were published about Soviet attempts to develop, with the help of sociologists, a new festal system, incorporating rituals of passage of the individual as well as public ceremonials, to serve as a basis for consensus (or for hegemony). As one writer put it, cultural management in the USSR had become a substitute for social revolution.[14]

The same basic preoccupation has informed social anthropology generally, the contribution of which should have been highly significant because of the discipline's methodology of holistic coverage, microscopic techniques and rigorous comparative perspective. However, even with these advantages, the endeavour has had to grapple with epistemological, methodological and theoretical difficulties because of the complexity of the problem and the multiplicity of variables involved. Perhaps the major difficulty is that the phenomena under consideration are both political and cultural simultaneously when these two broad components are themselves sharply different from one another. Another difficulty is the imprecise way in which the term 'culture' has been used. Even as early as the 1930s Kluckhohn and Kroeber found over a hundred different senses in which the term had been used.[15] Most intellectuals, as well as their informed audiences, would understand the term as

13. See A. Gouldner, *The Coming Crisis of Western Sociology*, London, Heinemann, 1971.
14. See C. Binns, 'The Changing Face of Power' (part 1), *Man*, 1979, pp. 585–606 and 'The Changing Face of Power' (part 2), *Man*, 1980, pp.170–87. See also C. Lane, 'Ritual and Ceremony in Contemporary Society', *Sociological Review*, 1979, pp. 253–78
15. See A.L. Kroeber and C. Kluckhohn, *Culture: A Critical Review of Concepts and Definitions*, New York, Vintage, 1952.

referring mainly to literature, drama, music, painting and the other fine arts generally. In most of his work on culture and politics, Raymond Williams uses the term culture in this sense. In his last book, *Culture*, he promises to deal with what he calls the anthropological sense of culture, but one looks in vain for this usage in his formulations.[16] Most anthropologists would agree with Marcuse that what Williams and other men of letters call culture consists of symbolic forms that are not only spontaneously expressive but are also instrumental, serving as techniques for staging what can be regarded as the core of culture, namely the values, norms, beliefs, symbols and ceremonials that govern interpersonal and intergroup relations.[17] Drama, music, dance, decorum and the like are frequently used as symbolic techniques in the ceremonials of kinship, religion, state occasions, and so forth. A great deal of their constraining power is derived from the obligatory nature of the relationships which they serve to instill.

Culture articulates for women and men two primary conditions for living: a measure of social order in the face of perpetually looming chaos and a semblance of stability in the face of perennial change and utter absence of predictability.[18] Society is a construction created by humanity and is precariously maintained by cultural institutions. Culture is rooted in human thought, in our physical and biological needs, and in our biographies through what are known as 'rites of passage'. In this way the psychic energy of the individual is activated to impel men to sustain and maintain the social order. Moreover, by linking the social system to the seemingly perpetual, relatively unchanging problems of human biology and biography, such as life and death, growth and decay, a degree of stability is secured for that order. Further stability and effectiveness are invested in the social system by the process of integrating the various strands of culture in such a way that if part of the resulting system becomes obsolete it will still be supported and maintained for some time by the other parts with which it is integrated.

An even more important process in this respect is the economy that is achieved in cultural symbols by charging the same symbolic form with several 'meanings' to serve different purposes within the system. This heightens the potency of the symbols as well as

16. R. Williams, *Culture*, p.19.
17. Marcuse, *The Aesthetic Dimension*, p.36.
18. See P.L. Berger and T. Luckman, *The Social Construction of Reality*, London, Allen Lane, 1967.

increasing the degree of their mystification. For example, ancestor worship in a patrilineal society such as the Tallensi, which takes ostensibly ritual form, is also a political activity because it reifies and maintains the genealogical order which articulates the division of the society into territorially-based lineages that are also economic and political groupings. It also defines and regulates kinship and affinity relationships and ritually explains fortune and misfortune affecting people.

Culture is thus instrumental in maintaining the web of social relationships in society. But these relationships are highly affected, if not shaped, by the distribution of economic and political power. Hence the struggle for power is also a struggle to attain control of the existing cultural forms to understand the underlying cultural forms and to introduce new cultural forms that will support the power holders that define, reify and support these relationships. As a result, nearly all cultural forms are politicised and contested. Culture reifies and helps to maintain the distribution of economic and political power in society.

For this reason Marx argued that the ideas of the ruling classes are in every epoch the ruling ideas. This was elaborately defined and developed by some of his followers, among them Althusser in his discussion of 'the ideological state apparatus' and members of the Frankfurt School in their analyses of the impact of mass media on modern society. Some writers have even credited the ruling classes with the creation not only of religion, but also of the multiplicity of such groupings as tribes and ethnic groups, and labelled scholars who studied these as 'ideologists' who, wittingly or unwittingly, reified such groupings and presented them as given 'in the nature of things', thereby in effect legitimising the established order. The central argument throughout is that the masses are made, through various techniques of instruction, persuasion and mystification, to accept and support the dominant culture and thereby indirectly to maintain the very politico-economic system that dominates and exploits them.

More recently, this monolithic view has been increasingly questioned and duly modified by some students of marxism, who have begun to analyse the nature of the sub-cultures that are developed by different sections of the subordinate classes in response and resistance to the dominant culture. This is a running theme in *Resistance Through Rituals*, written by members of the Centre for Contemporary Cultural Studies at the University of Birmingham.

126

The editors and some of the contributors to this work complain that the orthodox Marxian view 'treats the working class as the passive recipients of their culture and fails to trace the active process by which a culture is created from material experience'. In contrast, they would regard the subordinate subcultures as active responses by various oppressed groups to the hegemony of the dominant culture. This position is more explicitly discussed by Miliband in his book *Marxism and Politics*,[19] in which he states that account should be taken

> of the many-sided and permanent challenge which is directed at the ideological predominance of the "ruling Class", and the fact that this challenge, notwithstanding all difficulties and disadvantages, produces a steady erosion of that predominance. . . . This discussion of hegemony and class consciousness more than ever requires the inclusion of the concept of a battle being fought on many different fronts. . . The ideological terrain is by no means wholly occupied by "the ideas of the ruling class": it is highly contested territory.[20]

Social anthropologists had started their work from the other end of the social scale, by implicitly or explicitly attributing exclusiveness, even independence, to the small scale culture groups which they studied, and it was only after the independence of Third World countries, where they carried out their field studies, that they began to take account of the fact that those culture groups had been incorporated within larger nation-states whose dominant national ideologies impinged on them. In other words, particular cultures were now considered within the context of the nation-state. The analysis of the political nature of ethnicity, which began to gather momentum in the 1960s, has been one of the first outcomes of this orientation. The very definition of ethnicity in this view entailed interaction, often conflict, by culture groups within the nation-state. The process of this interaction was analysed in terms of politico-cultural dynamics, as political groups manipulated different types of cultural symbolic forms to articulate a number of basic organisational functions to coordinate their activities in the struggle for power.[21]

19. R. Miliband, *Marxism and Politics*, Oxford, Oxford University Press, 1977.

20. *Ibid.* pp.53–4. Also see S. Hall and T. Jefferson, *Resistance Through Rituals*, London, Hutchinson, 1975.

21. See A. Cohen, *Custom and Politics in Urban Africa*, London, Routledge & Kegan Paul Solidus, Berkeley and Los Angeles, University of California Press, 1969 and *Two-Dimensional Man*, London, Routledge & Kegan Paul Solidus, Berkeley and Los Angeles, University of California Press, 1974.

In the previous chapters of this monograph an attempt was made to examine Carnival as, in the words of Miliband, a contested territory. The balance of forces in that contest changes with circumstances. Carnivals generally are particularly suitable for exploring this issue, as their symbolic forms have the potentialities for political articulation, serving in some situations as 'rituals of rebellion' the effect of which is cathartic and ultimately a mechanism operating in the maintenance of the established order; in other situations they serve as an expression of protest, resistance and violence. Carnival is almost always precariously poised between these two extremes, invariably tense. At best it is like a grand 'joking relationship' which, as Radcliffe-Brown showed, is characterised by both conflict and alliance at one and the same time.[22] In this 'ideal type' of carnival, dominance and opposition are in a state of balanced equilibrium. To the extent that that balance is seriously disturbed, the nature of the festival would change and would thereby be transformed into a different form altogether. If the festival is made to express pure and naked hegemony, it becomes a massive political rally of the type staged in totalitarian regimes. If, on the other hand, it is made to express opposition, it becomes a political demonstration against the system.

In concrete historical reality the balance between the two tendencies is always uncertain, tilting in the one direction or the other to different degrees in response to political developments. The politico-cultural structure of the event is thus different from year to year. This was evident in the Notting Hill Carnival even during the second half of the 1970s when it was made politically radical, yet continued to some extent to have the structure of a joke with the established order. At times the joke was sour, sarcastic, bitter, but it was nevertheless there. For, despite Black Power rhetoric, and calls for exclusiveness and withdrawal and the ideology of the return to Africa, the majority of West Indians saw themselves as an integral part of British society, taking part in its institutions and benefitting from its social services. That love-hate relationship was nearly always expressed in the symbolic structure of the celebration. British kings, queens, bishops and Robin Hoods appeared alongside African liberation fighters and Rastafarian heroes in the same procession. At times, one masquerading theme combined the

22. A.R. Radcliffe-Brown, *Structure and Function in Primitive Society*, London, Cohen & West, 1952, pp.90–116. See also P. Burke, who describes carnival as being on a knife's edge, *Popular Culture in Early Modern Europe*, London, Temple Smith, 1978.

two motifs within the same theatrical form. Thus Sukuya's mas, 'Mansa Musa's Guests in Regina's Feast' in 1977, the jubilee year of the coronation of the Queen of England, represented a four-teenth-century West African king appearing with his entourage to celebrate the majesty of the British monarch.

Carnival's potentialities for political action are immense and are always exploited by power interests. In the first place, as many writers have pointed out, Carnival can be an integrative institution, helping to bring together in amity people from different classes and ethnic and religious groupings. This has tended to be the case in Trinidad since Independence, as the middle classes join the poorer sections and East Indians join Africans in the festivities so that the carnival became a symbol as well as an instrument of nationhood within a heterogeneous, potentially conflict-ridden population. The event can at the same time consolidate and help to institutionalise social hierarchy and, indirectly, the structure of authority within the polity. This was the case in Trinidad during the earlier part of the nineteenth century when Carnival symbol-ised and maintained a caste-like hierarchy on the island, as the white plantocracy staged their own carnival and although later allowing those of mixed colour to have their (separate) celebration prohibited the masses of slaves of African descent from taking part. In New Orleans in the United States, the carnival to this day asserts, in its organisation, procedure and dramaturgical structure, the supremacy of the aristocratic upper class within the city. Similarly, in the Rio Carnival in Brazil, the various bands, known as the Samba Schools, consist of masses of poor black working-class members who are artistically supervised and choreographed by white, middle-class, professional artists, while members of the upper classes assume the roles of judges in the competition between the bands, thus emphasising their leadership and supremacy in secular life and at the same time indirectly 'guiding' and controlling the dramatic themes that are enacted in the mas-querades.

Some anthropologists have emphasised, moreover, the so-called 'safety valve' function of Carnival, arguing that through the symbolic inversion of roles in the masquerade, as the world is stood upside down, when the ruled are allowed to masquerade as rulers in a ceremonial rebellion, people's pent-up bitterness and hostility against their masters are spent, in effect, thereby, strength-ening the political system and restoring social equilibrium. Other

writers have argued along the same line to the effect that the function of a carnival is to represent chaos and disorder, so dramatising
the importance of the return to order and sanity during the rest of
the year.[23] Thus, regimes have always seemed to orient carnivals
towards these integrative, ideologically hegemonous, authority-val-
idating functions.

However, as history repetitively demonstrates, a carnival's
potentialities for fostering criticism, protest, resistance, subversion
and violence are equally great; and at the best of times the celebration is poised between compliance and subversion. On the whole,
central authorities are always anxious to contain and even abolish
it, but once the tradition is established in a polity it becomes difficult for them to do so. It is only the most totalitarian regimes that
stop it altogether, as was the case in Spain under Franco, following
the civil war.

Carnival's possibilities for serving as an instrument for political
opposition are manifold. In the first place, the event is attended by
masses of people who substantially outnumber stewards and police,
and even in the most relaxed times are difficult to control. In the
history of nearly all carnivals there have been periods when the revelling masses have got out of hand and rioting has broken out.
People in groups become ecstatic, particularly when drinking alcohol or taking drugs, and when they happen to harbour grievances
against the established order they can easily be swayed to violence.

One conducive factor in this respect is personal anonymity,
achieved first and foremost by the ease with which an individual
fades within a crowd. Anonymity can also be achieved by masquerading. This is why in many carnivals the authorities prohibit
the wearing of face masks, as the British did in Trinidad during the
nineteenth century. In other cases, masking the face is allowed on
condition that the masker registers with the police, who give him a
serial number on his costume so that if he committs an offence he
will be identifiable by that number. In Notting Hill it was alleged
that pickpockets and trouble makers operated without fear during
the carnival, relying on the colour of their skin as a disguise. On
ordinary days throughout the year a black face could easily be spot-
ted in the predominantly white population. Indeed this 'cognition'
by colour alone had occasionally led the police to arrest and prose-
cute the wrong people. In the carnival this practice has been used

23. See Da Mata, 'Constraint and License', in S.F. Moore and B.G. Myerhoff,
Secular Rituals, Assen, Van Gorcum, 1977.

against the police. Thus, in a number of cases, the police alleged that when they had made an arrest on an ordinary day the accused threatened them, saying menacingly 'wait for Carnival day!'

The rioters in carnivals at times used as weapons some of the very implements traditionally used in play in the parade. In Trinidad, after the emancipation of the slaves, torches were used on the eve of the carnival, in celebrating 'Canbulay', the freedom festivity. On occasions when rioting broke out the torches were used to set buildings and police stations on fire. Eventually torches were prohibited by law. Again, one of the popular games in the Trinidad Carnival was stick fighting and on a number of occasions the sticks were used in assaults on the police and carrying them in the carnival was duly banned. In the Notting Hill Carnival in 1976, the tens of thousands of beer bottles from which carnival goers drank were used in sustained assaults on the police, of whom about 350 were injured; in subsequent years only canned beer was sold in the area during the carnival.

Another feature of carnivals that served opposition was the content of popular songs and the dramatic themes enacted by mas bands. In relaxed times, both conventions were used in humorous parodies of the centres of power; but on many occasions humour was easily swayed to satire, sarcasm, open criticism and incitement to violence. Bezucha surveyed a series of masquerades in France that used memiodramatic techniques in a silent agitation against the establishment of the day.[24] In the Notting Hill Carnival reggae lyrics and calypso songs were used to express bitter criticism and discontent with the police and racism.

What should be emphasised here is that conflict in carnivals is not accidental in the sense of only being an intrusion into an otherwise peaceful, politically neutral cultural form. Conflict is part of the very essence of the celebration. It is built into its very structure. This is why Carnival should be conceived as a kind of a joking relationship characterised by both alliance and enmity at one and the same time. Social anthropologists have documented the existence of such relationships in different contexts, such as the relations between in-laws, between wife-givers and wife-takers. In some preindustrial societies a mock battle is staged when the bride-takers come to the village of the bride-givers to take the bride, bringing

24. J. Bezucha, 'Masks of Revolution: A Study of Popular Culture During the Second French Republic', in R. Price (ed.), *Revolution and Reaction*, London, Croom Helm, 1975, p.53.

with them the marriage payment in the form of a herd of cattle. The bride-giving kin go out with sticks, menacingly hitting the cattle to drive them away, shouting at the visitors: we do not want your cattle and we do not want to give you our daughter. A ceremonial reconciliation follows but the tension continues, and is periodically alleviated by the compulsory observance of institutionalised forms of joking. A similar relationship exists in some societies between clans who are both allies and potential enemies. Joking in these cases is an institutionalised cultural mechanism for avoiding the flare up of open hostilities between potential enemies.

Carnival is a cultural mechanism expressing, camouflaging and alleviating a basic structural conflict between the state and the citizenry. To put it in terms of the Hobbesian mythology of the origin of the state, men and women, desirous of escaping from the chaos, uncertainties, perils and brutalities of the 'state of nature', agree to surrender part of their freedom to a centralised authority that will ensure law and order. But even when the state does not exceed its authority, men and women resent the limitations on their freedom and are always wary of their rulers, and the relation is always uneasy. Political systems differ in the ways this tension is treated. In many systems authority is ritualised, and is thus supported by the basic general concerns of the individual, such as life and death, fortune and misfortune, health and illness. In democratic regimes, secular legal procedures are available for the individual to complain, criticise and bring the authorities to court. In many societies ritual is used to mystify and regularly to resolve the conflict. When no such arrangements are institutionalised men may resort to violence against the existing regime, staging a rebellion or revolution. Carnival is another cultural mechanism staged in some societies as a ceremonial rebellion to alleviate this tension.

Carnival is thus politics masquerading behind cultural forms. When it is true to its form, combining conflict with alliance, 'pure culture' and 'pure politics' are melted down into a transcendental aesthetic unity.

1 0

The Aestheticisation of Politics

The polemic between the London Carnival leadership and the Arts Council during the 1970s was implicitly the perpetual philosophical controversy about the nature of the aesthetic. The Council, which gave strong support to such elitist art forms as the opera, ballet and the theatre could not see any aesthetic value in carnival masquerades, music, poetry and dance. It was only under political pressure that the Council conceded that carnival's arts could be assessed in accordance with Afro-Caribbean aesthetic norms and reluctantly agreed to give grants, relying on judgment by a committee of Afro-Caribbean artists.

The idea of the aesthetic, Eagleton argues,[1] began to assume great importance with the Enlightenment, when, with the rise of the bourgeoisie and increasing institutional differentiation, art works were detached from their social and cultural contexts and became commoditised, autonomous, self-determinate, free. These values were at the heart of the struggle of the middle classes for political hegemony, which explains why art assumes such importance for them. The ideological nature of the aesthetic, its supposed freedom and autonomy, reached perhaps its most extreme form in the philosophy of Kant who conceived it as an abstract principle similar to that of the moral categorical imperative: irreducible, irrefutable, self-created, unrelated to either human desires or political power. But Eagleton does not dismiss the concept altogether as sheer ideology. After all, it was a revolutionary concept in early capitalism because it liberated art from religion and from the aristocracy. He therefore tries to retrieve the positive elements in it and, in the light of formulations by Marx, Freud and Nietzsche, combines these elements with the body, its desires and sensualities.

1. Eagleton, *The Ideology of the Aesthetic*, Oxford, Basil Blackwell, 1990.

'I try . . . to reunite the idea of the body with more traditional political topics of the state, class conflict and modes of production, through the mediatory category of the aesthetic'.[2]

Generally, the debate about the nature of the aesthetic looms large in the discussion of so-called popular art and of the whole question of art and class formations. As the bulk of the carnival makers in Latin America, the Caribbean, New Orleans (USA) and in Notting Hill are not only poor but also disadvantaged descendants of former slaves, Carnival is categorised as 'popular culture', thus implicitly contrasting it with elite 'high culture', which is assumed to be pure, aesthetic, functionless, sheer form, detached from politics.

This conceptualisation and, more fundamentally, the whole question of class politics and the aesthetic can be clarified only through the analysis of concrete ethnographic cases. This is partly because of the imprecise nature of the concepts involved. The idea of Carnival is vague in both connotations and denotations and is difficult to operate with analytically, not only cross-culturally but also within the same culture. Even if the history of a carnival within the same society is ignored and the analysis is confined to one carnival in one year, ambiguity remains. A brief discussion of the Rio Carnival will clarify these issues. It will also raise the question of whether popular culture is an 'opium of the masses', inspired by the ruling classes as part of the dominant culture, whether it is a counter culture, an ideology of resistance and opposition, or whether it is a contested ideological terrain.

Carnival in Rio is celebrated by hundreds of bands of all sorts.[3] These bands fall into two major categories. The first consists of about forty bands known as the samba schools that are strictly formal, tightly organised, highly disciplined, closely watched and con-

---

2. *Ibid.*, p.7.
3. Probably the most detailed and illuminating literature on the Rio Carnival is in Portuguese. Most of Roberto Da Matta's authoritative work on the subject still awaits publication in English translation. The following account is based on publications in English, particularly those by Da Mata, 'Constraint and License', in S.F. Moore and B.G. Myerhoff (eds), and 'Carnival in multiple planes', paper given in Burg Warstenstein Symposium, no. 76 on Cultural frames and reflections, 1977; L.D. Gardel, *Escolas De Samba: A Descriptive Account*, Rio de Janeiro, Livraria Kosmos Editoria, 1967; A. Guillermoprieto, *Samba*, London, Jonathan Cape, 1990; J.M. Taylor, 'The Politics of Aesthetic Debate: The Case of Brazilian Carnival', *Ethnology*, vol. 21, 1982, pp.301–11; V.W. Turnes, 'Carnival in Rio', in F. Manning (ed.), *The Celebration of Society*, London (Canada), Congress of Social and Humanities Studies, 1983.

trolled by state agencies. The second consists of hundreds of bands that are informally and loosely organised, known as *blocos*.

On the three carnival days, the masses of tourists, politicians, journalists, celebrities, and other members of the Brazilian middle classes converge on the Sambadrome, where they fill the eighty thousand seats to watch the parade of the samba schools and follow the competition between them; the scene is also watched throughout live on television by an estimated audience of forty million Brazilians. As a result, a good deal is known about the samba schools, but very little about the hundreds of *blocos*,[4] and when people talk about the Rio Carnival they almost invariably have the samba schools' version of the celebration in mind.

The *blocos* are said to be spontaneous, authentic, grass roots, young, 'subversive'. Many of them seem to be ephemeral, lasting for one or two years, yet others are much more stable and sophisticated and might end up becoming samba schools, if they manage to overcome the series of obstacles that the authorities impose in the way of registering new schools. On the other hand, many *blocos* have recently been established by former samba school members, disaffected by the discipline, state control, commercialism and sexism of the schools.[5]

The samba schools are subjected to strict official regulations. They have to have an efficient organisation, should be run on sound business lines and should confine the themes of their masquerades to Brazilian history and Brazilian nationhood. Continuous supervision is exercised by Riotur, Rio's Department of Tourism. The schools are hierarchically ranked in three divisions on the basis of the marks they manage to score in the vigorous competition during carnival. They may be promoted or demoted in rank after every carnival. The competition is therefore intense and is motivated not so much by the quest for honour and prestige as by the financial gain attending success. The higher a school is in the hierarchy the more money it receives from different sources. Local and national politicians, celebrities, status seekers, business men, will all pay large sums of money for the honour of being seated in a prominent position on the leading float of the school during the parade. Also, some whites will pay a fee to join special sections among the dancers of a successful school. More money

4. Da Matta 'Carnival', gives an illuminating analysis of the structural differences between the Samba Schools and the *blocos*.
5. See Taylor 'Aesthetic Debate'; Turner 'Rio'.

135

comes from the sale of records of songs, television coverage, prizes, etc. The more money that comes in, the more professional, creative and competent the artists, choreographers, sculptors and media specialists that the school can hire to design its floats, to stage its general appearance and performance in the next carnival.

Thus there is a great difference between the carnival staged by the samba schools and that staged by the hundreds of *blocos*. Indeed, there are many Brazilians, including some members of the samba schools themselves, who question whether the Sambadrome three-day parade is a carnival at all. It looks more like an entertainment directed by the middle classes and ruling groups, using the masses of blacks as performers. The tedium of the patriotic dramatic masquerade themes is relieved by female nudity, colour and the infectious rhythm of the samba. Guillermoprieto writes of 'phalanxes of near-naked women, rotating their hips and smiling at the . . . audience which is understood to be white, male and in the market for dark flesh'.[6] She reports witnessing the first ever total nudity in the 1988 parade, exhibited by a woman appearing with one of the schools.

The schools' leaderships at times struggle with the authorities, but only over their share of the proceeds from admission fees at the Sambadrome and from television companies that cover the parade. In 1988 the schools succeeded in raising their cut on parade tickets to 40 per cent. In 1988 the cheapest seat at the Sambadrome cost US$40, equivalent to one month's minimum wage, and the price of a box went as high as US$16,000.[7] The extra money gained in this way helped in mounting yet more lavish floats in more sophisticated presentation in the next carnival while the black members of the school and their *favela* communities remained in poverty in their squalid slums and even continued to pay the bulk of the cost of their own costumes by instalments throughout the year. This is why the Rio Carnival is often dubbed the opium of the people.

This account may be balanced by the fact that the black masses participating nevertheless look excited and happy. But it is difficult to speculate over what goes on in their minds. The account given by Guillermoprieto, who was a participant observer with the Mangueira Samba School throughout the months of preparation for the 1988 carnival, indicates a great deal of anxiety, misery and tension experienced by the thousands of black carnivalists through-

6. Guillermoprieto, *Samba*, pp.181–2.
7. *Ibid.*, p.145.

out the season, as well as during the parade. Of the fully nude woman in the 1988 parade, Guillermoprieto states: 'It's hard to tell whether she is having fun. . . . Her smile is extremely practised, and her eyes look bewildered. Perhaps she knows how to dance but tonight she is moving carefully, stiff from the hips up, as if she were carrying a sandwich-board advertisement and pointing to the text: "See naked woman for free!"'[8] Of the hundreds of drummers, forming the *bateria*, without which a school cannot exist, she comments: 'They raise bloody welts on their shoulders from the drums' heavy straps, tearing the calloused skin on their hands with their ceaseless beating and rubbing of the metal instruments. . . . They never smile'.[9] As to the thousands of costumed members of the school, who are instructed by the rules of the samba to smile throughout, there is the lurking consciousness that success by the school might somehow reflect on the fortunes of their *favela*. There is constant pressure on the directorates of the schools to recruit as many masqueraders as possible, though it seems that in recent years the authorities decreed that the number should not exceed 2,500 for each school.

It is the schools, then, that provide the samba rhythm, the songs and the dance by the mass of costumed members, but the general dramatic framework within which these are contained and the aesthetic forms inspired by the media specialists, by Riotur officials, designers, artists, choreographers and by the jurors of the competitions are essentially white middle class. The establishment has truly stolen the show. The schools are also enmeshed in financial institutions and seem to be under continual political surveillance. The frequently cited samba school, 'the Mangueira', had as its president in 1988, a member of the state military police who was unpopular with the members of the school and was rumoured to have been involved in assassination squads and in drug trafficking. Guillermoprieto states that early in the season she went to ask his permission to monitor the school during the period of preparation for the carnival but that he declined. He was murdered a few days later and, although he was succeeded by his brother, she managed to cover the preparation for the celebration.

This brief account shows the ambiguity with which of the basically different types of celebrations enacted by the schools and by the *blocos* invest the term 'The Rio Carnival'. Further confusion

8. *Ibid.*, p.224.
9. *Ibid.*, pp.16–17.

arises if the term is also taken to encompass the history of the carnival, because today's samba schools were originally 'subversive' (i.e. out of control) *blocos*. Moreover there is the serious question of whether the schools' parade, as presented to the Brazilians and to the world as 'the Rio Carnival', is a carnival at all, and whether the overall aesthetic view is of the white middle class or the black under class, whether it is 'high culture' or 'popular culture'. According to Taylor's report, Brazilian intellectuals are currently asking such questions.[10] Her own tentative argument is that black and white aesthetics are integrated to make up a grand national symbol, legitimising the authority of the ruling class. Turner argues similarly: 'Brazilian culture has', he says, 'raised a traditional ritual of reversal to the scale of a great industrial nation'. He disarmingly describes the Rio Carnival as a 'dynamic, many-levelled, liminal domain of multiframed anti-structures and spontaneous communitas'.[11]

Similar transformations occurred in Trinidad's carnival when a frequently violent subversive ethnic Afro-Caribbean celebration was elevated after Independence into a state sponsored, middle-class dominated, tourist-oriented, national event. More recently the central celebration became a parade on stage, appearing before a seated audience and jurors, with emphasis on competition between the bands over such titles as King and Queen of the Bands, etc. In both the Rio and the Trinidad carnivals the aesthetic forms are essentially middle class. There was nothing 'popular' about Minshall's sophisticated 'Paradise Lost' which won the first prize in 1975.

Perhaps the issue of class and the aesthetic can be further examined by considering briefly an elitist carnivalesque movement that has developed, like the London Carnival, since the 1960s among purely middle-class Anglo Americans in California and which, according to recent reports, has now spread to many parts of the United States.

The reference here is to the 'Renaissance Pleasure Faire', sometimes described as 'California's Mardi-Gras', which is staged annually, for five weeks at a time, in Los Angeles in the spring, and in Marin County, north of San Francisco, in the summer. It is held by a not-for-profit cultural organisation called the 'Living History

10. Taylor 'Aesthetic Debate'.
11. Turner, 'Rio'.

Center' which is supervised by a Board of Directors. My account is confined to the Marin County scene, which I visited, though the programme seems to be essentially the same in Los Angeles.

Like carnivals, The Renaissance Pleasure Faire was a playful, frivolous affair, but, again like carnivals, there was behind all the masquerading, make belief, revelry and bawdiness, a motif whereby the past is revived to serve a collectivity of people as a myth for political action in the present. The faire was staged as a pure cultural event, reliving Shakespeare's times, with its music, arts, poetry, drama and play.

The faire was held in a meticulously reconstructed Elizabethan shire,[12] complete with shops, castle, six theatres, bakeries, breweries, washer women, dyers, tanners, herbalists, soothsayers, criers, jesters, masseurs, jewellers, dress makers and literally scores of other functionaries, typical of that exciting era in English history. Between 1,000 and 1,500 amateur and professional actors had been trained for a few weeks beforehand in the language and manners of the period and in playing different roles in running the faire town. The faire enthusiasts were invited to participate in pre-faire workshops where Elizabethan English was taught as a second language, research was conducted and costumes prepared. School children were introduced to the history of the Renaissance. All the actors and about half of the thousands of visiting revellers masqueraded in elaborately designed, academically-researched period costumes of a variety of social statuses, from noble men and women down to simple peasants. The organisation which ran the whole enterprise, would on request send to would-be participants an illustrated brochure teaching them how to make their own costumes, according to historical specifications. The majority of the masquerading visitors seemed to have bought their costumes from professional designers, though. One of the principles of the faire was that every object sold in its shops and kiosks should, like the pan of the steel band, be handmade. The craftsmanship displayed by the weavers, dressmakers, hat makers, candle makers, carvers, puppet makers, jewellers and others was masterly and executed with utmost taste and – again like the pan – the cost was inevitably high.

On a typical faire day between 15,000 and 20,000 visitors

---

12. Fictitiously located somewhere on the border between Oxfordshire and Buckinghamshire. See G. Duncan, *The Shire: A Traveller's Guide to Our Village and its Environs*, Novato, Celebration Press, 1979.

attend. On the occasions when I attended the shire town was very much part of the landscape of the Black Forest at Novato and as one approached it from the highway, permanent official road signs indicated the turning. This led to a gigantic car parking area where traffic was regulated by wardens who communicated via walkie-talkies. As one approached the shire one was greeted by a brass band playing period music. At the entrance there was an Information Office where posters, maps and guide to the faire, as well as history and literary books dealing with the Renaissance period, were sold. When one entered the shire, one, in effect, stepped back four centuries, into a pleasant world of make believe. The dramaturgical reconstruction was astonishing, with criers chanting in Elizabethan English the wares of their kiosks, the washerwomen slapping the clothes on the edge of the fountain and singing throughout the day, men and women engaged in different types of traditional games, and so on. At the entrance to each of the six open-air theatres a poster gave the repertoire of the day. The visitors to the faire were part of the drama; one of the slogans of the faire organisers was: 'the whole faire's a stage'. All spoke, or attempted to speak, in Shakespearean English.

There was a great deal of eating – particularly barbecued turkey legs eaten by hand as might have been the manner of King Henry the Eighth had he been familiar with the meat – and there was also a great deal of ale drinking, of kissing, dancing, bawdiness, revelry and singing. Through all this the crowds moved from one type of activity to another, watching each other, playing, eating, resting, attending theatrical performances, strolling through the numerous kiosks, sampling handicrafts and watching craftsmen at work. Periodically throughout the day organised parades by bands of costumed men and women moved from one end of the town to the other. They represented different social groups in Elizabethan society, 'including the barbarous Highlanders of Scotland and Ireland', and were accompanied by traditional music bands.

The day's programme culminated, late in the afternoon, with the Royal Procession, starting at 3.00 p.m. to be exact. Queen Elizabeth, fully crowned, jewelled and attired was carried in a sedan, preceded by bellringers and musicians and followed by a multidudinous, fully-costumed entourage of ministers, nobility, guards, attendants, jesters and dancers as well as loyal subjects. The procession passed through the shire and stopped at the grand spacious theatre where crowds of visitors and revellers had installed themselves waiting on seats in the form of compressed haystacks arranged in rows facing the large stage. The overflowing crowds seated themselves on the surrounding slopes of hilly terraces.

Good Queen Bess alighted from the sedan and entered the theatre from its back, followed by the rest of the procession. The entire crowd of spectators rose to their feet, and in a serious, emotionally-charged tone shouted in unison 'God Save the Queen; God Save the Queen'.

From two sides the queen and her followers climbed the stairs to the vast and complex stage, which had a fixed reproduction of a part of a sail ship on one side. In an upper floor over the stage there were couriers, a brass band and the operators of sound effects, such as a large metallic sheet which helped reproduce the sound of a sea storm. An expert in hand sign language stood on the right-hand side of the stage conveying the dialogue to the deaf.

The crowd resumed their seats and there followed a performance, lasting for over an hour, of a play, and of a play within the play, dominated by the theme of the struggle for hegemony between England and Spain, with the audience being drawn into the performance by booing the Spanish commanders and cheering Captain Drake and his navy. Special emphasis was placed on Drake's pioneering visit to California, more specifically – in accordance with some historical evidence – to Marin County, where he and his companions were treated by the local Indians as gods who had come from the world beyond. Drake duly claimed the land for Queen Elizabeth.

The play within the play was a parody and was done with much vulgar humour, showing how Drake had crossed the ocean to defy the Spanish claims that they alone had ruled the waves. King Philip of mighty Spain appeared on stage and was greeted with hisses as he declared: 'To rule the world is my aim; and crush old England and its Queen'. This was followed by the entrance into the centre of the stage of the queen saying: 'I am Elizabeth; this realm shall I defend; and pray to heavens a hero to me to send; to stop proud Spain so that England and her shores stay free'. Wild cheers from the audience greeted her speech and Francis Drake eventually came to the rescue, defeated the enemy and was knighted by the queen amidst much rejoicing – among the audience as well as on stage. Towards the end of the performance the whole audience joined in singing: 'Long may she reign in majesty glorious; ever victorious; God save the Queen'. Elizabeth responded finally by saying:

'Good my people; I have reigned with your love; my life and reign shall be for your good. Never shall you have another sovereign who loves you more'.

This is only a short sketch of what was a highly pleasurable experience. The faire gave the appearance of being yet another example of what Umberto Eco calls 'Hyper Reality', an American obsession with realism, 'where, if a reconstruction is to be credible, it must be absolutely iconic, a perfect likeness, a "real" copy of the reality being represented. . . where the boundaries between game and illusion are blurred'.[13] It certainly was that, but the faire was not just a detached museum piece, self-contained, irreducible. Behind the 'illusion' was a political reality in the here and now in California.

First, almost all of the many thousands who attended the event were Caucasian. One hardly saw any of the variety of skin colour that would be seen in great numbers in the streets of nearby San Francisco. The few individual black faces that were in evidence were those of members of the amateur or professional groups of actors employed by the faire. Secondly, the crowds were obviously financially well off. (Marin county was sometimes described as 'a middle-class white ghetto'.) One could not attend without having a private car. The daily entrance fee alone in 1981 was US$9 per person, though a season ticket cost only US$25. Food and drinks, without which the experience, the 'trip into the past', could not be properly lived, cost a good deal of money. Even a kiss cost a few dollars. Meanwhile for the thousands who attended in costumes, the expense could have reached several hundred dollars each. Though a peasant's costume was cheap, not many peasants could be seen around, most of the masqueraders went for costumes of higher statuses.

Thirdly, it is fair to assume that this was an educationally sophisticated audience, as without a knowledge of what the Renaissance period was and some understanding of the symbolism of the whole affair, the experience could not have meant anything. Indeed, many members of the audience seemed to have gone to the trouble of learning some of the language of the period and among the audience of the grand performance many seemed to know verbatim some of the passages of the play. The message of the celebration was further consolidated by other related events organised by the Living History Centre throughout the year for

13. U. Eco, *Travels in Hyper Reality*, London, Helen and Kurt Wolffe, 1986.

adults and also for children in schools where, according to the organisers, hundreds of thousands of children were involved.

Fourthly, from conversation with participants in the faire and outside it, it appears that many, if not most of the audiences were men and women who identified with English culture, often claiming to being English in origin. But for third or more generation immigrants to assume an exclusive English descent, a double uni-lineal English descent, through both father and mother, resulting from absolute endogamy within the group, ought really to be demonstrated. This, however, is difficult to establish and most people seemed to claim having only one or two remote links with an English ancestor. An English identity under these circumstances would seem, therefore, to be more of an achieved than of an ascribed status. It was achieved through the adoption of certain life styles and ideologies as well as taking part in specific cultural performances like the Renaissance Faire. A living History Center leaflet is headed: 'Celebrate your Heritage. Become a Living History Center Enthusiast'. The leaflet goes on to point out that The Living History Center is not only recreating the Renaissance. It *is* the Renaissance. . . . Our heritage is a precious legacy. Treasure it; celebrate it, perpetuate it as a Living History'.

From talking to a few Renaissance Faire enthusiasts, it was evident that the faire experience was not confined to the actual visit to the faire but lingered long afterwards in conversations, in the display of the handicraft objects bought from the faire, in wearing the faire's costumes on some occasions[14] and perhaps in attending other performances of English themes, such as the Dickens Christmas Faire staged, again, by the Living History Center. Indeed the Center claimed that the Renaissance Pleasure Faire had popularised English cuisine and had also revolutionised handicrafts throughout California. All this is not just make believe; it is a subtle process of self manipulation and shaping of consciousness, in which Californians in particular seem to be so skilled.

The Renaissance Faire was started in Los Angeles in 1963 and in Marin County in 1968. To appreciate its political significance it must be considered in relation to other politico-cultural movements that had been developing at the same time in California and

---

14. In Cyra McFadden's 1977 novel, *The Serial*, which portrays Marin County social and cultural life, the heroin, Kate, wore her Renaissance Faire costume to a wedding, even though she felt mildly ridiculous in it, 'but it wasn't so bad without the conical hat' (p.7).

elsewhere in the United States. Foremost among these movements was the Civil Rights Movement, the rise of Black Power. The 1960s seem to have put an end to the melting pot ideology in American sociocultural history and to have ushered in a variety of ethnic movements, involving tens of millions of people. As a part of the same process, another time-honoured piece of ideology that suffered was the principle that equated Americanism with Anglo-Saxonism.

Those developments were particularly challenging in California, where Anglo-Saxon culture was not as firmly established as on the East Coast and where more challenging politico-cultural movements operated. Prominent among such movements was that of the Hispanics, the Spanish speaking groups, consisting overwhelmingly of Mexican Americans, whose number had been increasing dramatically as a result of continued immigration, both legal and illegal.[15] There are probably a million and a half Hispanics in Los Angeles alone while they now comprise nearly a fifth of the total population of California and there are some people who predict an Hispanic majority in the Golden State by the turn of the century.

The Mexican Americans have been organising for concerted political action on federal, state and local levels, clamouring for benefits and for cultural and linguistic distinctiveness. In California they demand their 'natural rights' in the land as original settlers, as, until the middle of the nineteenth century, the state was part of Mexico. They insist on having their children educated bilingually, in Spanish as well as in English. Alarmed 'Anglos' believe the Hispanics are 'out to create a separate state'.[16] Apart from the ethnic divide, there was also an overlapping class divide, with the Mexican Americans being essentially unskilled or semi-skilled labourers. Class differences and conflicts were thus fed into ethnic differences and conflicts.

It is against this political background that the symbolism of the Renaissance Pleasure Faire can make sense. In The Play the Hispanics' claim that California was theirs is rebutted by the Anglos' assertion that the Englishman, Drake, was there first, when he claimed the land for the Queen of England. The political issues involved were serious concerns, but were couched in the form of a

15. For some details see G. Cohen, 'Alliance and Conflict Among Mexican Americans', *Ethnic and Racial Studies*, vol. 5, no. 2, 1982, pp.175–95 and 'The Politics of Bilingual Education', Oxford Review of Education, vol. 10, no. 2, 1984, pp.225–41.

16. See G. Cohen 'Alliance and Bilingual Education'.

joke because the Mexican Americans were United States citizens and were contributing to the country's economy by their labour. In other words the relation between the two sides was a combination of cooperation and conflict. Furthermore, an elitist group cannot organise as such within a liberal democracy and has therefore to resort to subtle informal organisational strategies for raising consciousness of identity and exclusiveness, maintaining communication between members.

Both the Notting Hill Carnival and the Renaissance Pleasure Faire were frivolous, playful, merry-making cultural occasions that involved masquerading, excessive eating and drinking, mobile sections and stationary ones, with the stall holders playing a major cultural part. Both attempt to serve also as a celebration of a 'transition' in nature. The Notting Hill Carnival marked the end of summer; in California the faire celebrated the coming of spring in the Los Angeles event and the end of summer in the Marin County event. Both were concerned with establishing an identity and unity among disparate individuals and groups to confront present day political challenges. Both emphasize the need to educate the young about the ideology and performance involved.

They differed in other respects, though. While the carnival was held in the open, the Renaissance Faire was enclosed and exclusive, as in most elite celebrations.[17] The costumes that the masqueraders wore in the Renaissance Faire might have been true to historical specifications, but artistically they were dull and unimaginative when compared with many of the Notting Hill Carnival costumes, particularly those of the queens and kings of the bands, which, like African masks or Picasso's paintings, excited the imagination and made the observer think and wonder about the meaning of the strange unusual shapes and mysterious characters they conjured up. There was no ambiguity about the Renaissance Faire's masques. They represented established power, authority, tradition and status. Their 'meaning' was clear. The message of the faire was that the politico-economic status quo must be defended, that continuity must be ensured.

The Notting Hill Carnival on the other hand was an openended movement, both politically and culturally and was continually unpredictable. Its central message, what Marcuse would call

17. See A. Cohen, *The Politics of Elite Culture: Explorations in the Dramaturgy of Power in Modern African Society*, Berkeley, University of California Press, 1981.

'its hidden categorical imperative',[18] was that things ought to change. Some of the traditional European carnival characters *did* occasionally appear in some of the mas bands, such as 'fancy sailors' and 'midnight robbers', but this was a rarity. A great deal of creativity was displayed year after year in new creations. Until the late 1980s the carnivalists resisted the 'professional guidance' of British middle-class artists. In contrast, these have become the arbiters of artistic forms in the Rio and Trinidad carnivals.

Which is 'high art' and which 'popular art' in this situation, seems to be irrelevant. Essentially the same celebratory form could achieve the same end for the privileged as for the under class. In both cases the event is culturally expressive and politically instrumental. The Renaissance Pleasure Faire was not 'autonomous', 'irreducible', 'free' after all.

The Carnival concept is a highly flexible formula that encompasses different forms within the genre, and the same celebration may change from one form to another in the course of its history. Thus, the Notting Hill Carnival was initially staged as a traditional fair, later changed its form to that of a traditional-type carnival, then, with the rise of the stall holders around stationary sound systems, it developed into a complex form, combining the features of both fair and carnival. Such metamorphoses in the form of the celebration are always interrelated with political developments.

Both the Renaissance Pleasure Faire and the Notting Hill Carnival were conceived in dramaturgical terms. The organisers of the Renaissance Pleasure Faire regarded the whole faire as a stage and the people attending it as actors. Similarly, the carnivalists regarded carnival as 'Theatre of the Street' and all revellers as actors. In each, culture and politics were melted down into a transcendental aesthetic unity.

The foregoing discussion has dealt with different forms within the carnivalesque genre: the parade of the samba schools, the spontaneous chaotic celebration of the *blocos*, the elitist experience of the Renaissance Pleasure Faire, the different forms the Notting Hill Carnival displayed at different periods in its history. Each form is an aesthetic unity of politics, culture and what Eagleton calls the body.[19] But this transcendental unity, with its autonomy and

18. H. Marcuse, *The Aesthetic Dimension*, London, Macmillan, 1979.
19. Eagleton, *Ideology of the Aesthetic*.

authenticity, is never completely realised; it is continually subverted by the dynamics of power relations. Marcuse refers to the dual meaning of art, as aesthetic form and as technique. The aesthetic form is essential to its function as technique. Aestheticisation is thus a process continually converting content into form, as Marcuse would put it.[20] In this process rational politics is converted to non-rational cultural forms, the non-moral to the moral, the desires of the individual to the duty towards the collective, particularity to universality.

20. Marcuse, *Aesthetic Dimension*.

Conclusion

The Notting Hill Carnival has been presented and discussed as a politico-cultural movement. In such a movement a collectivity creates, revives, modifies, mobilises and integrates various cultural forms to deal with rapidly changing economic-political conditions. The evolving cultural structure defines the political identity and exclusiveness of the collectivity, serves as a system of communication between its members, uniting them and providing them with an ideology to guide their action. In the process the cultural forms undergo a transformation by being ceremonialised, ritualised, aestheticised, mythologised and thus appear as autonomous, irreducible, signifying functionlessness, detached from politics.

Cultural forms cater for fundamental biological, psychological, social and metaphysical necessities in our lives. In the process they create, symbolise and objectify a measure of order, and make up the 'reality' which we inhabit, the natural as well as the social, in the face of ever impending chaos and continuous flux, thus making it possible for us to conduct our daily life with a degree of certainty. We accept this 'reality' as habitual, traditional, commonsensical. This is the case in all societies, everywhere.

But in complex, pluralistic, class societies there are, in addition, contesting versions of reality, with each major political group attempting to develop a definition of reality that will enhance and consolidate its power. A dominant group seeks to develop hegemony by presenting its version of reality as the authentic one, but is often challenged by opposition groups, which under some circumstances rise in the form of cultural movements. Thus the battle to reshape culture is often also a battle over power. This is clearly demonstrated in religious movements, from the revolutionary at one extreme end to the ultra-conservative at the other.

When for some reason the hold of an articulating cultural form on people weakens, a movement develops to delineate and authenticate a substitute form. Thus when ethnicity was denounced as a divisive principle, whether in newly independent African states or in the United States during the 'melting pot' period, many ethnic groups transformed themselves into religious groupings.[1]

Again, Eagleton discusses how the rise of English literature from about the middle of the nineteenth century compensated for the decline of the old religious ideology in providing the principal integrating cultural form within the British polity.[2] Literature dealt with universal human values, conveyed timeless truths and was detached from history. Like religion it worked by emotion and by dramatic enactment rather than by abstract argument. It communicated subtle moral values and was the supremely civilising pursuit, the most central of all disciplines, immeasurably superior to law, science, politics, philosophy or history. It cultivated individualism, yet enhanced nationalism and solidarity between social classes. It pacified the deprived by providing vicarious fulfilment of unsatisfied desires.

Among the West Indians in Britain the most important form in their culture was music. Since the days of slavery it had been their major articulating cultural form. We asked a large number of men and women of different ages among them the question 'What is West Indian culture?' and the overwhelming majority unhesitatingly singled out music, often associating with it dance, poetry and rap. Music indeed pervaded their social life all the time, serving as a vehicle for communication of information, for comment on current affairs, for organising resistance and struggle. Even the poorest of West Indian households spent a great deal of money on buying sophisticated electronic equipment to play music throughout the day and well into the night. A casual observation of their youth in the streets and clubs of the inner cities would not fail to display vibrant creativity in developing ever new forms of music, lyrics, dance, mime, rap in response to current political developments. Music aesthetics saturated their life.[3] The carnival developed and

1. See A. Cohen, *Custom and Politics in Urban Africa*, London, Routledge & Kegan Paul, Berkeley and Los Angeles, University of California Press, 1969 and *Two-Dimensional Man*, London, Routledge and Kegan Paul, Berkeley and Los Angeles, University of California Press, 1974.

2. T. Eagleton, *Literary Theory: An Introduction*, Oxford, Basil Blackwell, 1983, pp.17–53, passim.

3. See D. Hebdige, 'Reggae, Rastas and Rudies', in S. Hall and T. Jefferson (eds), in *Resistance Through Rituals*, London and Birmingham, Hutchinson, 1975 and *Cut 'N' Mix*, London, Comedia Books, 1987; S. Jones, *Black Culture, White Youth*, London, Macmillan Education, 1988.

integrated the different islands' musics and thus mobilised the masses of West Indians into the movement.

It is essential to point out that what is being called here 'the articulating cultural form' does not exhaust the whole culture of a group. Nor does it comprehend the whole political organisation of the group because, in time, all the other component forms of the culture become politicised and thus contribute to some extent to the overall political strategies of the collectivity. It would therefore be more accurate to talk, for example, of 'a predominantly religious ideology', taking ideology to refer to the whole politicised culture. Furthermore, the various cultural forms differ in their potentialities for political articulation. Religion is still a significant factor in the maintenance of the political system in Britain; English literature is not a politically perfect substitute. The different forms of culture have different potentialities for articulating different parts of political organisation. Only the comparative analyses of detailed ethnographic studies of cultural movements can clarify these issues.

One of the central analytical problems in the analysis of politico-cultural dynamics is how rational political strategies are transformed into non-rational, non-political cultural forms. I first discussed this issue in a detailed study of the rise of an Islamic mystical order called the Tijaniyya among the members of a Hausa trading community who lived in an exclusive quarter called Sabo within the Yoruba city of Ibadan in Nigeria.[4] In a lengthy critique of that work, Laitin,[5] a political scientist, argued that I had somehow fudged the issue by resorting to a functionalist argument, finding 'solutions' to problems but no 'solvers'. He contended that the analysis of politico-cultural causation requires an explanation of the part played by 'rational choice' in bringing about the transformation. A brief discussion of the case would help in clarifying this central issue.

Under the umbrella of the British colonial administration, known as 'indirect rule', the Sabo community had succeeded in developing an ethnic polity that enabled the Hausa to establish a monopoly of long-distance trade in certain commodities between

4. Cohen, *Custom and Politics* and *Man.*
5. D.D. Laitin, 'Rational Choice and Culture: A Thick Description of Abner Cohen's Hausa Migrants', in F. Eidlin (ed.), *Constitutional Democracy: Essays in Comparative Politics*, Boulder: Westview, 1983 and *Hegemony and Culture*, Chicago and London, University of Chicago Press, 1990.

the north and the south of Nigeria, in the face of stiff competition with Yoruba traders. But, with the demise of indirect rule and the eventual independence of Nigeria, ethnicity was declared 'public enemy number one' and Sabo was no longer recognised as a distinct political entity, and the authority of its chief was undermined and its control of the trade was thus seriously threatened. It was at this juncture that the community adopted the Tijaniyya order and, within two years, transformed itself into a distinct and exclusive puritanical religious brotherhood, thereby reintegrating corporately and restoring the authority of the chief by the support of a new ritual hierarchy. The vehicles for that transformation were the thousands of regular divinatory sessions between laymen and the religious clerics, whose help was constantly sought concerning every contingency in daily life.

In these sessions laymen expressed their current problems and anxieties to the clerics who, in the frequent theological meetings they held among themselves, pooled their information about the current problems that afflicted their clients. The clerics were permanently settled in the quarter and had their own observation of what was going on in business and in other fields of social life and their ritual diagnoses were almost certainly affected somehow by this secular knowledge and they would thus have injected minor doses of 'rational choice' into their ritual prescriptions. A more direct and important element of rational choice was made at the top, when the leading clerics and the trade lords met together with the chief to discuss more general communal problems.

Rational choice is thus involved in the leadership process, which is a collective function, not a matter of arbitrarily acting individuals. The leading clerics of Sabo did not act capriciously when they initially chose to be initiated into the Tijaniyya; they had been conscious of the current problems of the community. Likewise the members of the community were not simpletons who could be duped into joining the order if they were not convinced that the order was propitious for them.[6]

Similar processes were involved in the rise of the English literary movement in Britain in the last century. Most of the Romantic poets were themselves political activists and so combined political rationality with literary creativity.[7] Rational political choice was

6. Full details can be found in Cohen, *Custom and Politics.*
7. Eagleton, *Literary Theory,* p.20.

151

transformed into poetry that was 'as opaque to rational enquiry as the Almighty himself: it existed as a self-enclosed object, mysteriously intact in its own unique being'.[8]

Similarly, in the London carnival movement, many of the participating musicians and artists were also political activists, and the leading political activists were at the same time committed carnivalists. The calypsonians, the reggae singers, the sound systems' toasters, regularly converted political issues into songs and rhythms that were experienced as intrinsic aesthetic creations in their own right. The Renaissance Pleasure Faire was originally 'invented' by two drama professors and has since been cultivated further by other 'leaders', including academics. It is important at this point in discussing the processes of politico-cultural dynamics to distinguish between the original creation or adoption of a new cultural formulation and its dissemination among the membership of the collectivity. While the formulation may be the creation of a single individual, a poet, composer, rap artist or calypsonian its efficacy depends on the extent of its impact on the collectivity. Abercrombie *et al.* seem to be referring to this process by the term 'apparatus of transmission' which every theory of ideology should specify.[9] In the Hausa case discussed above, the major apparatus was the divinatory session. Among the West Indians in London there was a plurality of apparatuses: sound system sessions, poetry reading sessions, calypso performances, etc.

In a different context, these politico-cultural sessions were called 'the crucial politico-symbolic drama', referring to such a recurring major cultural performance as the Friday midday prayer in Muslim societies when, in the obligatory presence of all the adult males of the community including the ruler and chief Imam, and amidst ritual communion with God, a sermon is given directing the faithful to fulfil their religious duties, such as waging jihad (holy war), which is one of the five pillars of the faith, against current enemies.[10] This is often not a once-and-for-all event, but is a continual process of interpretation and reinterpretation of modification or recreation, in the course of which new rational choices are injected into the ideology in response to current political developments.

A potentially articulating cultural form is successful only to the

8. *Ibid.*, p.47.

9. Abercrombie *et al.*, *The Dominant Ideology Thesis*, London, George Allen and Unwin, 1980, pp.1578.

10. See Cohen, *Man*, pp.131–4.

extent of its acceptance by the members of the collectivity; otherwise it would mean nothing to them and they would eventually reject it. Thus, an increasing number of members of the samba schools in Rio resent the hegemonous ideology and aesthetic norms that middle-class artists, media specialists and officials of Riotur impose on them. Abercrombie *et al.* argue that in late capitalism the dominant ideology has been effective only within the dominant class itself and is far from having been the powerful cement that integrated the whole society in the way the Frankfurt school, Althusser and others had argued; what integrates capitalist society is sheer division of labour.[11] The Renaissance Pleasure Faire attracts and is meaningful to only Anglo-Americans, although it is meant to be an All-American concern.

However, one cannot be dogmatic on this point by adopting one extreme thesis or the other, but one can heuristically regard them as the two ends of a continuum along which different cultural movements can be located, allowing for possible changes of position over time. In other words, it would be more accurate to treat cultural forms as 'contested territories', tilting to one side of the continuum or the other as the case may be.

Thus, after the emancipation of the slaves in Brazil in 1881, the Rio Carnival became a resistance and an opposition black movement. Later, many black carnivalists were forced to organise in the form of the samba schools and thus the official celebration became national, virtually part of the dominant ideology of the ruling class. The *blocos*, on the other hand, remain ethnic and potentially subversive, resisting the dominant ideology, but their existence remains precarious. A similar process can be seen in the history of the Trinidad Carnival.

The Notting Hill Carnival, is likely to develop, if it survives the formidable obstacles to its continued existence, into a predominantly tourist-oriented show. Already the police-delineated framework and the organisational and financial prescriptions of the Coopers & Lybrand Report are steering the event in that direction. The CEC is bracing itself to the phasing out of public institutional financial support. To improve the chances of the bands to attract sponsorships of businesses a marketing company has been hired to improve the public image of the carnival by dissociating it from its violent past. An indication of what can be achieved in this respect can be seen in the success of Ebony steel band which, after win-

11. Abercrombie, *et al.*, *Dominant Ideology*.

ning the Notting Hill Panorama Championship in 1983, was sponsored by the Jamaican Brewery, Red Stripe Lager. The band changed its name to Red Stripe Steel Band and embarked on advertising performances in a number of European countries and that led to greater success and fame in Britain.

A cultural movement is *ipso facto* also a political movement. Carnival may ostensibly appear to be a pure cultural performance, but it is inevitably political from the start. As a celebration of release from the constraints of the social order it would attract those who are under endless pressure, the dispossesed and the oppressed. It might function as a cathartic safety valve at times, but unavoidably it soon becomes a security problem calling for the active intervention of the forces of law and order. If the problem does not degenerate quickly the state may attempt to co-opt it, thus, in effect, politicising it on a higher level for its own benefit.

As a cultural movement evolves, it generates overlapping interpersonal networks of amity among the people actively involved in it and thus infuses the cultural form with moral imperatives, thereby consolidating and strengthening its central force. Thus in the Notting Hill Carnival, organisers, mas men, steelband men, sound system men, calypsonians, pan makers, costume designers, the Mangrove leadership, prominent stall holders, competition jurors, the local lawyers who stand ready to deal with the police and the courts in cases arising from the carnival, these and many others, who are in fact the central force of the carnival movement have, over the years, known each other in face-to-face interaction, so forming a far-flung network of amity relationships whose moral categorical imperatives added another source of constraint to pursue the cause.

A cultural movement would soon clash with the dominant culture, whether this is rooted in consensus or in the interests of the politically dominant group. This group would try to contain the movement by incorporating it within its structure. The movement would thereby become contested politically as well as culturally, on a continuum from a predominantly resistance movement to a predominantly coopted one. Thus a carnival movement may succeed in realising its main goals or may end up becoming an opium of the masses, a cathartic mechanism serving as a safety valve which may even be inspired and cultivated by the dominant group in its bid for hegemony.

A cultural movement is always entangled with other movements and the first task in its study is to identify, delineate and analytically isolate it. The Notting Hill Carnival movement, for example, embraces many movements, such as those of the steel bands and Rastafarianism, each of which can be isolated for intensive study on its own. Similarly, the Renaissance Pleasure Faire movement embraces a good deal of the environmentalist movement.

The comparative study of cultural movements can be most conveniently carried out in the city. There is no point here in raising the vexed question of whether there are special sociological principles governing urban life that are distinct from those governing rural life. Hypothetically, a cultural movement such as that of the Notting Hill Carnival can arise in both type of society, though it is obvious that the movement described in this monograph is fundamentally urban in its form, content and scale. The music is specifically crowd and street music and its impact has been dramatic because of urban density in which masses of black and white people lived in close proximity. In Notting Hill the noise of the loud music of steel bands and of sound systems is within ear-shot of the palatial homes of the wealthy in the surrounding streets. The ever present danger of rioting flaring up can spill out into neighbouring streets or provoke the National Front into confrontation.

One feature of the urban environment that facilitates the study of politico-cultural movements is rapid change, enhanced by intensity of interaction between interest groups competing and struggling for economic and political power daily. Thus, in a matter of only a few years a cultural movement such as that of steel band music, started, developed, spread, matured and became a powerful symbol, as well as an instrument, used by the West Indians in their struggle. This rapid change provides ideal heuristic conditions for the study of politico-cultural dynamics, as the process is conveniently telescoped in time and space for sociological exploration. In addition, a movement in the city proceeds in the full glare of recorded publicity, thus offering the investigator extensive data that can be corroborated with evidence from observation, interviews and from other sources of information to throw more light on the central problematic of the relation between culture and politics.

Bibliography

Abercrombie, N. *et al.* 1980 *The Dominant Ideology Thesis*, London: George Allen and Unwin

Althusser, L. 1971 'Ideology and Ideological State Apparatuses', in *Lenin and Philosophy*, New York: Monthly Review Press

Anderson, P. 1976 *Considerations on Western Marxism*, London: NLB

Anwar, M. 1991 'The Context of Leadership', in M. Anwar and P. Werbner (eds.) *Black and Ethnic Leaderships*, London and New York: Routledge.

Austin, H. 1979 'Carnival: Reflections on a Community', *New Community*, no.7, pp.114–17

Barrett, L.E. 1977 *Rastafarianism*, London: Heinemann Education

Benedict, B. 1983 *The Anthropology of World's Faires: San Francisco's Panama Pacific International Exposition of 1915*, Berkeley and London: Scholar Press

—— 1991 'International Exhibitions and National Identity', in *Anthropology Today*, vol.7, no.3

Berger, P.L. and Luckman, T. 1967 *The Social Construction of Reality*, London: Allen Lane

Bezucha, J.B. 1975 'Masks of Revolution: A Study of Popular Culture During the Second French Republic', in *Revolution and Reaction*, Roger Price (ed.), London: Croom Helm, p.53

Binns, C. 1979 'The Changing Face of Power' (part 1), in *Man*, pp. 585–606.

—— 1980 'The Changing Face of Power' (part 2), in *Man*, pp.170–87.

Black Peoples Progressive Association, *et al.* 1978 *Cause for Concern: West Indian Pupils in Redbridge*, Ilford: Black Peoples Progressive Association and Redbridge Community Council

Burke, P. 1978 *Popular Culture in Early Modern Europe*, London: Temple Smith

Cagnoni, R. 1975 'The Carnival is Over', *Sunday Times Magazine*, 20 April, p.14

Cashmore, E. 1977 'The Rastaman Cometh', *New Society*, pp.382–4

—— 1979 *Rastaman: The Rastafarian Movement in England*, London: Allen & Unwin

Chase, L. 1978a, *Notting Hill Carnival – Street Festival*, London: private-ly published

—— 1978b *The Power and the Glory*, London: privately published

—— 1979 *Streets of Chance: The Future of Multicultural Society*, London: private publication

Cohen, A. 1969 *Custom and Politics in Urban Africa*, London: Routledge & Kegan Paul; Berkeley and Los Angeles: University of California Press

—— 1974 *Two-Dimensional Man*, London: Routledge & Kegan Paul; Berkeley and Los Angeles: University of California Press

—— 1981a *The Politics of Elite Culture: Explorations in the Dramaturgy of Power in a Modern African Society*, Berkeley: University of California Press

—— 1981b 'Variables in Ethnicity', in *Ethnic Change*, C.F. Keyes (ed.), Seattle: University of Washington Press, pp.306–31

Cohen, G. 1982 'Alliance and Conflict Among Mexican Americans', in *Ethnic and Racial Studies*, vol.5, no.2, pp.175–95

—— 1984 'The Politics of Bilingual Education', in *Oxford Review of Education*, vol.10, no.2, pp.225–41

Cohen, S. 1991 *Rock Culture in Liverpool*, Oxford: Clarendon Press

Crowley, D.J. 1956. 'The traditional masques of Carnival', *Caribbean. Quarterly*, 3 and 4 pp.194–223

Da Mata, R. 1977a 'Constraint and License', in *Secular Rituals*, S.F. Moore & B.G. Myerhoff (eds), Assen: Van Gorcum

—— 1977b 'Carnival in multiple planes', paper given in Burg Wartenstein Symposium, no. 76 on Cultural frames and reflections.

Dodd, D. 1978 'Police and Thieves on the Streets of Brixton', *New Society*, pp.598–600

Duncan, G. 1979 *The Shire: A Traveller's Guide to Our Village and its Environs*, Novato: Celebration Press

Eagleton, T. 1983 *Literary Theory: An Introduction*, Oxford: Basil Blackwell

—— 1990 *The Ideology of the Aesthetic*, Oxford: Basil Blackwell

Eco, Umberto. 1986 *Travels in Hyper Reality*, London: Helen and Kurt Wolffe

Edmonson, M.S. 1956 'Carnival in New Orleans', *Caribbean Quarterly*, 3 and 4, pp.233–45

Esslin, M. 1977 *Brecht's Choice of Evils*, London: Heinemann

Frankenberg, R. 1957 *Village on the Border*, London: Tavistock

Gardel, L.D. 1967 *Escolas De Samba: A Descriptive Account*, Rio de Janeiro: Livraria Kosmos Editoria

Gilmore, D. 1975 'Carnival in Fuenmayor', *Journal of Anthropological Research*, no. 31, pp.331–49

Gluckman, M. 1942 *Analysis of a Social Situation in Modern Zululand*, Manchester: Manchester University Press

Gould, T. 1979 'The Mangrove Seven', *New Society*, January pp.5–6

157

Gouldner, A.W. 1973 *The Coming Crisis of Western Sociology*, London: Heinemann

Guillermoprieto, A. 1990 *Samba*, London: Jonathan Cape

Gramsci, A. 1971 *Selections from the Prison Notebooks*, Q. Hoare and G.N. Smith (ed. and trs.), London: Lawrence & Wishart

Hall, S. and Jefferson T. (eds.) 1975 *Resistance Through Rituals: Youth Subcultures in Post-War Britain*, London: Hutchinson

Hebdige, D. 1975 'Reggae, Rastas and Rudies', in *Resistance Through Rituals*, S. Hall and T. Jefferson (eds.), London and Birmingham: Hutchinson

—— 1979 *Subculture: The Meaning of Style*, London: Methuen

—— 1987 *Cut 'N' Mix*, London: Comedia Books

Hill, E. 1972 *The Trinidad Carnival: Mandate for a National Theatre*, Austin and London: University of Texas Press

Horkheimer, M. 1974 *The Eclipse of Reason*, London: Oxford University Press

Howe, D. 1976 'Is a Police Carnival', *Race Today*, vol. 8, no. 9, pp.173–5

—— 1977 *The Road Make To Walk On Carnival Day*, London: Race Today Publications

—— 1988 *From Bobby to Babylon*, London: Race Today Publications

Howe, I. 1957 *Politics and the Novel*, Cleveland: Meridan Books

Huizinga, J. 1955 *Homo Ludens*, Boston: Beacon Press

Jones, S. 1988 *Black Culture, White Youth*, London: Macmillan Education

Johnson, B. 1985 *I Think of My Mother*, London: Karia Press

Johnson, L.K. 1976 'The Reggae Rebellion', *New Society*, 10 June, p.589

—— 1977 'Jamaican Rebel Music', *Race and Class*, pp.397–412

Jones, S. 1988 *Black Culture, White Youth*, London: Macmillan Education

Kitzinger, S. 1969 'Protest and Mysticism', *J.sci.Stud.Relig.* no.8, pp.240–62

Kroeber, A.L. and Kluckhohn, C. 1952 *Culture: A Critical Review of Concepts and Definitions*, New York: Vintage

La Rose, M. 1990, *Mas in Notting Hill*, London: New Beacon Books

Laitin, D. D. 1983, 'Rational Choice and Culture: A Thick Description of Abner Cohen's Hausa Migrants', in F. Eidlin (ed.), *Constitutional Democracy: Essays in Comparative Politics*, Boulder: Westview

—— 1990 *Hegemony and Culture*, Chicago and London: The University of Chicago Press

Lane, C. 1979 'Ritual and Ceremony in Contemporary Soviet Society', *Sociology Review*, pp.253–78

Lee, T.R. 1977, *Race and Residence*, Oxford: Clarendon Press

Macinnes, C. 1971 'Mangrove Trial', *New Society*, 23 December: p.1261

MacDonald, J.S. and MacDonald, L. 1978 'The Black Family in the

Americas: A Review of the Literature', *Sage Race Relations Abstracts*, no. 3, pp.1–42

Manning, F.E. 1977 'Cup Match and Carnival', in *Secular Ritual* S.F. Moore and B.G. Myerhoff (eds.), Amsterdam: Van Gorcum

—— 1978 'Carnival in Antigua', *Anthropos*, no. 73, pp.191–204

—— 1983 'Cosmos and Chaos: Celebration in the Modern World', in F.E. Manning (ed.), *The Celebration of Society*, London (Canada): Congress of Social and Humanistic Studies

Marcuse, H. 1964 *One–Dimensional Man: The Ideology of Industrial Society*, London: Routledge & Kegan Paul

—— 1979 *The Aesthetic Dimension*, London: Macmillan

Marx, K. and Engels, F. 1970 *The German Ideology*, London: Lawrence & Wishart

McFadden, C. 1977 *The Serial: a Year in the Life of Marin County*, New York: The New American Library

Miliband, R. 1977 *Marxism and Politics*, Oxford: Oxford University Press

Mintz, S.W. 1974 *Caribbean Transformations*, Chicago: Aldine

Mitchell, C. 1956 *The Kalela Dance* (Rhodes-Livingston Paper no. 7) Manchester: Manchester University Press

Nettleford, R.M. 1970 *Mirror, Mirror*, Kingston: William Collins & Sangster

Noel, T. 1978 *The Steelband*, London: The Commonwealth Institute

Owens, J.V. 1978 'Literature on the Rastafari: 1955–1974', *New Community*, no.6, pp.150–64

Peacock, J.L. 1968 *Rites of Modernisation*, Chicago: University of Chicago Press

Pearse, A. 1956 'Carnival in Nineteenth Century Trinidad', *Caribbean Quarterly*, no.3 & 4, pp.175–93

Pearson, D.G. 1977 'West Indian Communal Associations in Britain', *New Community*, vol.5

Peters, E.L. 1963 'Aspects of Rank and Status Among Muslims in a Lebanese Village', in *Mediterranean Countrymen*, J. Pitt-Rivers (ed.), Paris: Mouton

Phillips, M. 1976 'Behind the Frontline', *Daily Mirror*, 1 September

Pilger, J. 1976 'Behind the Frontline', *Daily Mirror*, 1 September

Pilkington, E. 1988 *Beyond the Mother Country*, London: I.B. Tauris

Powell, E. 1969 *Freedom and Reality*, Kingswood: Elliot Right Way Books

Powrie, B.E. 1956 'The Changing Attitude of Coloured Middle Class Towards Carnival', *Caribbean Quarterly*, no.3 & 4, pp.224–32

Pryce, K. 1979 *Endless Pressure*, Harmondsworth: Penguin Books

Radcliffe-Brown, A.R. 1952 *Structure and Function in Primitive Society*, London: Cohen & West

Rotberg, R. 1961 'The Lenshina Movement of Northern Rhodesia', *Rhodes-Livingston Journal*, no.29, pp.63–78

Select Committee on Race Relations and Immigration, 1977 *Report on the West Indian community*, London: HMSO

Smith, M.G. *et al.* 1960 *The Ras Tafari Movement in Kingston, Jamaica*, Mona: University College of the West Indies

Sollors, W. 1978 *Amiri Baraka/Le Roi Jones*, New York: Columbia University Press

Stadlen, F. 1976 'The Carnival is Over', *Times Higher Educational Supplement*, 26 November

Stellman, M. 1974 'Sitting Here in Limbo', *Time Out* no.234, pp.11–13

Taylor, J.M. 1982 'The Politics of Aesthetic Debate: The case of Brazilian Carnival', *Ethnology*, vol.21, pp.301–11.

Taylor, R.L. 1978 *Art, an Enemy of the People*, Hassocks: The Harvester Press

Troyna, B. 1977 'The Reggae War', *New Society*, 10 March, pp.491–2

Turner, V.W. 1957 *Schism and Continuity in an African Society*, Manchester: Manchester University Press

—— 1974 *Dramas, Fields and Metaphors*, Ithaca and London: Cornell University Press

—— 1983 'Carnival in Rio', in F. Manning (ed.), *The Celebration of Society*, London (Canada): Congress of Social and Humanities Studies

Walker, M. 1977 *The National Front* London: Fontana/Collins

Warner, K. 1982 *The Trinidad Calipso*, London, Kensington, Port-of-Spain: Heinemann

Werbner, P. 1991 'Black and Ethnic Leaderships in Britain', in M. Anwar and P. Werbner, *Black and Ethnic Leaderships*, London and New York: Routledge

Wickenden, J. 1958 *Colour in Britain*, London: Oxford University Press

Williams, R. 1979 *Politics and Letters: Interviews with New Left Review*, London: NLB

Williams, R. 1981 *Culture*, London: Fontana

Wilson, B. 1973 *Magic and the Millennuim*, London: Paladin

Wintour, P. 1977 'Bored Enough to Riot', *New Statesman*, September pp.291–2

Wood, D. 1968 *Trinidad in Transition*, London: Oxford University Press

Newspapers and Journals Quoted

Daily Mail

Friends

Guardian, the

The Independent

Kensington News

Kensington Post

The *KN* and *KP* were orginally two separate papers. Later they were merged, for the first few years under the title *KPN*. Eventually the *P* was dropped and now it is called *KN*.

New Society

New Statesman

Observer

Notting Hill Carnival

Race Today

Sunday Times

Telegraph

Times

Westindian World

West London Observer

Index

Subject Index

163